# WHY WE NEED CONFESSION

# WHY WE NEED CONFESSION

## Russell Shaw

Our Sunday Visitor Publishing Division
Our Sunday Visitor, Inc.
Huntington, Indiana 46750

*Nihil Obstat:*
Rev. William E. Lori, S.T.D.
Censor Deputatus

*Imprimatur:*
✝James A. Hickey
Archbishop of Washington
October 29, 1985

The Nihil Obstat and Imprimatur are official
declarations that a book or pamphlet is free of
doctrinal or moral error. No implication is contained
therein that those who have granted the Nihil Obstat
and the Imprimatur agree with the contents,
opinions, or statements expressed.

International Standard Book Number: 0-87973-537-6
Library of Congress Catalog Card Number: 85-63153

*Cover design by James E. McIlrath*

PRINTED IN THE UNITED STATES OF AMERICA

537

# ACKNOWLEDGMENTS

Scripture quotations in this work are taken from the *New American Bible*, © 1970 by the Confraternity of Christian Doctrine, Washington, D.C., and are used by permission of said copyright owner. No part of the *New American Bible* may be reproduced in any form without permission in writing from the copyright owner. All rights reserved. The author is also grateful to the copyright holders of various works (mentioned throughout this book) from which short quotations have been excerpted, especially to the Costello Publishing Company, Inc., for the use of brief excerpts taken from *Vatican Council II: The Conciliar and Post-Conciliar Documents*, © 1975 by Costello Publishing Company, Inc., and Rev. Austin Flannery, O.P., general editor. If any copyrighted materials have been inadvertently used in this book without proper credit being given, please notify Our Sunday Visitor Publishing Division, Our Sunday Visitor, Inc., in writing so that future printings of this work may be corrected accordingly.

# Contents

# INTRODUCTION

## What This Book Is and Isn't

There are many things this book is *not*. It isn't a systematic exposition of the theology of sin and the sacrament of penance; it isn't a history of the sacrament; it isn't a treatise on spirituality; it isn't a polemic against those who hold other views on the matters discussed here. It is not even an argument for returning to the "good old days."

This book is an attempt to explain why Catholics who either no longer receive the sacrament of penance or seldom receive it are making a mistake. Its intention is to encourage those who no longer go to confession to resume doing so, those who confess occasionally to confess more often, and those who already know the benefits of frequent confession from experience to share what they've learned.

I have consulted a number of works in

preparing this book, most notably Pope John Paul II's apostolic exhortation *Reconciliatio et Paenitentia* (Reconciliation and Penance). I owe a special debt of gratitude, however, to Dr. Germain Grisez, whose *Way of the Lord Jesus, Volume One: Christian Moral Principles* (published in 1984 by the Franciscan Herald Press) has been an invaluable source of a number of the ideas expressed throughout this work. I recommend it highly to those interested in a more detailed explanation of these ideas.

— *R.S.*

# CHAPTER 1

# What's Happened to Confession?

Why don't Catholics go to confession any more?

The question, of course, overstates the case. Many Catholics *do* receive the sacrament of penance, and quite a few receive it regularly and frequently. Penance remains an important element in their spiritual lives.

But the question also corresponds to a reality visible in parishes throughout the United States and, apparently, in other countries as well. Long confessional lines are a thing of the past. Many Catholics receive penance very seldom and some perhaps not at all.

One recent study of Catholic life in the United States found that among "core Catholics" — those who identify with parishes — 27% never go to confession, 35% receive the sacrament only once a year, 33% several times a year, and only 6% monthly or more often. Even among "parish leaders," 15% never go to confession and 33% only once a year. Somewhat optimistically, the authors of the study remarked that the sacrament of penance "remains part of being a Catholic in the practice of nearly three-quarters of those with parish connections." True enough — but, for most, not nearly as *large* a part as it used to be.

Why?

Any reasonable answer must give due recognition to the fact that the situation in the past wasn't an unmixed blessing in all respects. There is reason to believe that, for some Catholics at least, frequent confession was something of a rote exercise. Indeed, for some it had overtones of scrupulosity. Thus the case for frequent confession has to be based on something besides returning to the not-so-good old days.

But the move away from confession during the last two or three decades merely represents a different kind of excess. Common sense suggests that it has complex causes.

I was chatting with some Catholic friends not long ago when one of them made a rather surprising statement. "I don't believe in original sin," he said. "I mean, that's that stuff about Adam and Eve. It's mythology. I don't buy it."

So much for several millennia of Christian and Jewish belief. So much for the Old and New Testaments. So much for one of the cornerstones of the Redemption. Relegated to the category of myth. That settles that.

Or does it?

As a matter of fact, merely saying "I don't believe" doesn't settle anything. Sin — whether original sin or personal sin — is either real or it's not. If it's not, no harm is done by denying it. But if "original sin" and "personal sin" are dangerous realities, denying them makes them still more dangerous, much as denying the reality of a serious illness increases the chances that you'll die from it.

I don't cite my friend's remark in order to criticize him. He, after all, was only voicing sentiments a lot of other people probably share these days. He was being more honest than most.

Original sin is one thing, though, and personal sin is something else. People still believe in personal sin, don't they? Or do they? A few years ago, the title of a psy-chiatrist's book attracted a good deal of at-tention: *What Ever Happened to Sin?* The implication was that, however painfully aware people might be of the evil in the world, many were increasingly disinclined to blame themselves for it.

Fish on Friday, Latin in the Mass . . . and sin. By and large, the first two have van-ished from contemporary Catholic life. As for sin, the jury is still out.

In October 1983, over two hundred bish-ops and other Church leaders from around the world convened at the Vatican to discuss such matters as these. The sixth general as-sembly of the international synod of bishops focused on the theme "Reconciliation and Penance in the Mission of the Church." A lit-tle over a year later, Pope John Paul II pub-lished his own document on the subject. In it he summed up the deliberations of the synod and added his own thoughts.

As this suggests, the "disappearance" of sin from the contemporary Church — or, to be more accurate, from the thinking of many contemporary Catholics — is a matter of high-level concern. My friend's comment, typical of many these days, provides grist for this mill. Evidently there is a need to sort out the issues and see what's at stake.

Bring back sin? We could do worse. For without a clear grasp of the reality of sin, it's hard to see much chance for reconciliation. "To acknowledge one's sin," Pope John Paul observes, "indeed . . . to recognize oneself as being a sinner, capable of sin and inclined to commit sin, is the essential first step in returning to God."

Then why do so many people apparently have doubts about sin?

One reason may be that too much was made of it in the past. To a considerable extent, religion seemed to be largely a matter of avoiding sin and religious practice a way of staying on God's good side. Love, joy, celebration — these things tended to get lost in the shuffle.

Often enough, morality was reduced to legalism. It was presented as a set of rules, a code: don't miss Mass on Sunday, don't steal, don't commit adultery. All this was sound, and it was based on divine revelation; but it was not self-explanatory. There was a pervasive sense of guilt. Sin and damnation

15

seemed to lurk around every corner, and Saturday-night confession was as integral a part of popular Catholicism as Sunday-morning Mass.

Simple-minded "demythologizing" has also played a part in what has happened, and here, as my friend's remark suggests, belief in original sin has been particularly hard hit. Except for fundamentalists, few people these days take the story of Adam and Eve in Genesis altogether literally. It doesn't follow, though, that the Adam and Eve story does not correspond to a real event and is not telling a profound truth about humanity; yet many people, anxious not to appear naïve, seem to have lost sight of the truth which it embodies.

In his document on reconciliation and penance, the Holy Father recognizes these and other problems (including secularization and a faulty understanding of behavioral sciences) which help account for the weakening of the sense of sin. And he acknowledges that the problems come from within the Church as well as from outside it.

"For example," he remarks, "some are inclined to replace exaggerated attitudes of the past with other exaggerations: from seeing sin everywhere they pass to not recognizing it anywhere; from too much emphasis on the fear of eternal punishment to preaching a love of God that excludes any punishment deserved by sin; from severity in trying to correct erroneous consciences they pass to a kind of respect for conscience which excludes the duty of telling the truth.''

What is the truth? It might be stated this way: if our greatest dignity as human beings resides in the fact that we can be saints, our second greatest dignity paradoxically concerns the fact that we are sinners. Dangerous and destructive as sin is, recognizing sin is an acknowledgment of our freedom and responsibility, and any acknowledgment of these contains the seeds of something better.

In this respect our situation, as suggested earlier, is not unlike that of a man with a dangerous disease. If he recognizes that he's sick, he may be able to do something about it; but if he refuses to acknowledge his illness, the outlook isn't good.

That is why explanations of evil which try to account for it apart from human freedom are, in their way, threats to our well-being and assaults on our dignity. The case with us is very much as it is with children; their efforts to deny wrongdoing or shift blame to others are signs of immaturity which, if prolonged, become cause for concern; but when children start taking responsibility for their misdeeds, they have begun to grow in moral maturity.

From this point of view, the problem with the tendency of Catholics and others to downplay sin is that it places an obstacle in the path of growth. Emotional maturity and holiness aren't identical, but they do converge in this: we grow when — and only when — we accept responsibility for what we freely choose to do.

To one who examines the proceedings of the 1983 bishops' synod or reads Pope John Paul's apostolic exhortation, it is clear that their intent isn't to overemphasize sin and guilt or present a legalistic view of morality. The positive aspects of Catholic experience in the last quarter of a century are taken for granted.

But it is also clear that the bishops and the pope are worried. Excesses of a different kind have flourished in the last twenty-five years. Many people have largely lost sight of sin, impaired their capacity for growth, and placed themselves in a perilous situation. The need now is to strike a proper balance between dwelling too much on sin and trying to ignore it entirely.

The discussion of sin is inseparable from the discussion of the sacrament of penance (or simply reconciliation, as it is often called), whose special role in Christian life is the forgiveness of sin. Yet even while approaching penance from this perspective — sin — we must not lose sight of the sacrament's role in the positive pursuit of sanctity. The next few chapters will stress the dark side, but after that we shall turn to the good news.

# CHAPTER 2

# The Problem of Evil

Where does the evil in the world come from and how can it be corrected? Human beings past and present have devoted a vast amount of time and attention to those questions, on whose answers depend matters of great practical importance.

Several competing answers are abroad today. Among them are these:

• *The therapeutic explanation.* The evil in the world comes from disorders of the human psyche, and these disorders can be treated by the techniques of therapy. According to this view, what we call evil is the product of illness, and the evil will disappear as illnesses are cured.

• *The consumer explanation.* Evil is defined as not having enough material goods to cushion one against a harsh world. The solution is to amass wealth and the security it brings. In its benign form, this approach admits that wealth and possessions should be shared equitably so that everyone will enjoy as much security as possible. In its selfish form, it concentrates on individual or class acquisitiveness, with little or no concern for others.

• *The revolutionary explanation.* The evil in the world is the result of unjust political, economic, and social systems. The solution is to replace oppressive systems with systems which are just. Since those who benefit from the present state of affairs can be expected to resist change, it must be brought about by violent revolution.

• *The educational explanation.* The evil in the world arises from ignorance. People do the wrong thing because they literally do not know any better. Education will solve the problem by supplying them with knowledge and, in the form of science and technology, directing their energies into productive channels instead of destructive ones.

To be fair about it, one has to admit that each of these explanations contains a good deal of truth.

The therapeutic explanation is correct in

22

saying that much misery arises from disorders of the psyche. To the extent that therapy contributes to integrating conflicting elements of personality, it can indeed be helpful.

The consumer explanation is correct in saying that much suffering comes from lack of material goods. While it is hard to find much good to say about merely selfish consumerism, the altruistic version which admits the need for a more equitable distribution of wealth points to an urgent problem and its realistic solution.

The revolutionary explanation rightly notes that oppressive political, economic, and social systems add much to the misery in the world. The solution of violent revolution, which usually ends by replacing one oppressive system with another, must be rejected as an authentic answer on both pragmatic and Christian grounds. Still, the analysis is accurate as far as it goes.

The educational explanation is correct in saying that people make many blunders, which do injury to themselves and others, simply out of ignorance. Such errors can indeed be prevented by education, which substitutes knowledge for ignorance and truth for falsity.

In conceding the partial correctness of these four explanations, nevertheless, one comes finally to the conclusion that none is adequate either as an account of evil or as a prescription for remedying it. We know from experience that there is evil which has its origins not in illness, poverty, unjust systems, or ignorance, but somewhere else. It is important to understand why.

To one degree or another, all four views — therapeutic, consumer, revolutionary, and educational — fall short by not taking seriously, or seriously enough, the role of freedom in human life. The therapeutic explanation does this by confusing moral evil with sickness. The consumer explanation does it by equating evil with the lack of material wealth and good with its possession. The revolutionary explanation does it by situating evil in "systems" and attempting to eradicate it only by substituting new systems for old. The educational explanation does it by identifying evil with ignorance and proposing to eliminate it by replacing ignorance with knowledge.

While each of these views speaks a certain truth and must be taken seriously, none takes adequate account of human freedom and its contribution both to evil and its eradication. At the root of much of the misery in the world lie abuses of freedom: in other words — moral evil, or sin.

This is one of the central themes of Pope John Paul II's post-synod document on penance and reconciliation. Of particular interest is his treatment of "social sin" on the one hand and personal sin on the other.

The concept of "social sin" has been much discussed in recent years, and I shall have more to say about it here a little later. The expression refers to an important reality, namely, the suffering caused by unjust social structures and systems which trample on human rights and ignore human needs.

As the Holy Father points out, though, "social sin" is not self-explanatory. Where do unjust structures come from? What keeps them in existence? His answer — of crucial importance — is that they are created and sustained by personal sins. Thus his prescription for fundamental, lasting social reform is personal penance and reconciliation.

For, as he remarks, "At the heart of every situation of sin are always to be found sinful people."

That is not to dismiss the need for efforts directed to political, social, and economic reform. (Pope John Paul certainly does not.) It is merely to call attention to the fact that social sin is "the result of the accumulation and concentration of many personal sins" and must necessarily be confronted on that level.

Underlying this is an insight which is central to virtually everything the pope says: the dignity of each human person. Paradoxical as it may seem, it is essential to the defense of individual dignity to acknowledge the fact of personal sin, and *not* submerge it in impersonal "systems" and "structures" or confuse it with sickness or psychic disorder as contemporary explanations of evil often do.

Plainly, then, there is an urgent need today to recapture what Pope John Paul calls "a healthy sense of sin." Sin is not a very pleasant subject, but, if we are to cope realistically with the fact of sin in and around us, we must have an accurate understanding of what sin is and how to deal with it. The subject is more complicated than it may seem at first, since the one word "sin" actually refers to several different realities. In the next chapter we will see what some of these are.

# CHAPTER 3

# Original Sin and Personal Sin

How are we to regain "a healthy sense of sin"? In the first instance, evidently, by recapturing a correct understanding of what sin is. That requires looking first of all at both original sin and personal sin.

"Original sin," the American Protestant theologian Reinhold Niebuhr once remarked, "is the only empirically verifiable doctrine in Christianity." Whether or not that's literally the case, the quip expresses a crucial fact: evidence abounds that there is something fundamentally out of whack with the human race.

What is original sin? Part of the doctrine concerns a moral calamity which occurred at the dawn of history — a primal act of rebellion against God by our first parents, a rebellion whose very disorder and bitter consequences are transmitted from generation to generation. This is what the story of Adam and Eve expresses.

But the doctrine also concerns our present experience of original sin. Perhaps this is best understood as human nature as it now comes to us — flawed, troubled, at odds with itself. Saint Paul describes the symptoms: "I cannot even understand my own actions. . . . What happens is that I do, not the good I will to do, but the evil I did not intend. . . . My inner self agrees with the law of God, but I see in my body's members another law at war with the law of my mind; this makes me the prisoner of the law of sin in my members" (Romans 7:15-23).

Like Paul, we are aware of this "dis-integrity" in us, an interior conflict which often leads to external deeds causing conflict with other persons. It is easy to say one doesn't believe in original sin; it is impossible to deny that one experiences its consequences.

Cardinal John Henry Newman gave testimony to this insight in his classic statement of faith, the *Apologia pro Vita Sua.* Surveying the evil in the world ("a vision to dizzy and appal"), he concluded that the evidence "inflicts upon the mind the sense of a profound mystery, which is absolutely beyond human solution."

What shall be said to this heart-piercing, reason-bewildering fact? I can only answer, that either there is no Creator, or this living society of men is in a true sense discarded from His presence. Did I see a boy of good make and mind, with the tokens on him of a refined nature, cast upon the world without provision, unable to say whence he came, his birth-place or his family connexions, I should conclude that there was some mystery connected with his history, and that he was one, of whom, from one cause or other, his parents were ashamed. Thus only should I be able to account for the contrast between the promise and the condition of his being. And so I argue about the world; — *if* there be a God, *since* there is a God, the human race is implicated in some terrible aboriginal calamity. It is out of joint with the purposes of its Creator. This

is a fact, a fact as true as the fact of
its existence; and thus the doctrine of
what is theologically called original
sin becomes to me almost as certain
as that the world exists, and as the existence of God.

This, we may suppose, is the same reality of which Saint Paul writes in his epistle to
the Romans (3:9-20):

Well, then, do we find ourselves in
a position of superiority? Not entirely.
We have already brought the charge
against Jews and Greeks alike that
they are under the domination of sin.
It is as Scripture says:
"There is no just man, not even
one;
there is no one who
understands,
no one in search of God.
All have taken the wrong course,
all alike have become
worthless;
not one of them acts uprightly,
no, not one.

Their throats are open tombs;
  they use their tongues to
    deceive;
The venom of asps lies behind
    their lips.
Their mouths are full of curses
    and bitterness.
Swiftly run their feet to shed
    blood;
  ruin and misery strew their
    course.
The path of peace is unknown to
    them;
  the fear of God is not before
    their eyes."

We know that everything the law says is addressed to those who are under its authority. This means that every mouth is silenced and the whole world stands convicted before God, since no one will be justified in God's sight through observance of the law; the law does nothing but point out what is sinful.

The doctrine of original sin is necessary (as an explanation) from at least two points of view. First, it is necessary if we are to understand the reason for the Incarnation and the Redemption. Why, to put it simply, should God have gone to so much trouble? Ultimately, of course, the answer is love, and we cannot hope to fathom God's love. Yet we can easily enough understand that God would *not* have gone to such lengths — would indeed have had no reason to — if the human race were not in a desperate situation arising from sin.

"Because [Man] has fallen," C.S. Lewis writes, "for him God does the great deed; just as in the parable it is the one lost sheep for whom the shepherd hunts. Let Man's preeminence or solitude be one not of superiority but of misery and evil: then, all the more, Man will be the very species into which Mercy will descend." Saint Paul expresses this succinctly: "Therefore, just as through one man sin entered the world and with sin death, death thus coming to all men inasmuch as all sinned . . . much more did the grace of God and the gracious gift of the one man, Jesus Christ, abound for all" (Romans 5:12, 15).

Second, the doctrine of original sin is

necessary to give an adequate account of the empirical facts of human "dis-integrity" and inclination to evil of which Newman, Niebuhr, Paul, and many others speak, and of which all of us are keenly aware in our own lives. I say the doctrine is *necessary* from this perspective on the assumption (which it is beyond the scope of this book to demonstrate) that human beings possess freedom of choice. If one accepts an exclusively deterministic account of human nature, of course, one will not agree that human beings are free, nor need one then account for the human predisposition to evil except on some such grounds as a flaw in the evolutionary process.

Curiously enough, however, from both points of view it is only the doctrine of original sin — and certainly not the evolutionary, deterministic account — which entitles us to take a hopeful view of human destiny. As G.K. Chesterton once said, original sin signifies that "we have misused a good world, and not merely been entrapped into a bad one. It refers evil back to a wrong use of the will, and thus declares that it can eventually be righted by the right use of the will." Were one not to believe this, the evidence of evil and inclination to evil in humanity would be a strong, indeed compelling, reason to despair. But as matters stand for the Christian, "it is precisely in this that God proves his love for us: that while we were still sinners, Christ died for us" (Romans 5:8).

* * *

The difference between original sin and personal sin is something like the difference between a congenital abnormality and a self-inflicted injury. Original sin comes with the turf — our flawed human nature. Personal sin is our own doing, the particular contribution each of us makes to the sum total of evil in us and around us.

There are various ways to express the reality of personal sin — disobedience to God, violation of the moral law, and so forth. One way which brings home sin's "personal" character is to understand sin as an injury we do ourselves.

Some of our sins visibly hurt other persons. If I steal from someone, I harm him by taking what belongs to him. Most people have no difficulty accepting the idea that this is wrong.

In other cases, nobody else is directly, visibly injured (though every sin, even the most hidden, to some degree harms relationships between the sinner and other persons). That's especially true of interior sins: thoughts and desires. I decide to commit a theft, make my plans and preparations, and then at the last minute — deterred perhaps by fear of being caught and punished — do nothing. Nobody gets hurt. How is it that a "sin" has been committed?

In fact, however, somebody *has* been directly hurt — myself. The nature of the injury becomes clear when we consider what transpires in such a case.

First and foremost, sin is a choice. Morally speaking, however, we make ourselves the sort of people we are by our choices. A person who chooses (that is, intends) to act heroically makes himself a hero; a person who chooses to act lovingly makes himself a loving person. This is so even if an individual never has the opportunity to perform deeds which correspond to his noble choices.

And it is also true in the case of sinful choices. One who chooses to steal makes himself a thief; one who chooses to lie makes himself a liar; one who chooses to lust makes himself a lustful person. Obviously the situation is worse when people carry out such choices in action. Then, usually, somebody else *does* get hurt. But even if there is no external deed corresponding to the choice, the act of choosing by itself defines the moral identity of the person who makes it, and sin harms the sinner.

Thus Paul, in Romans 6:15-23, speaks of sin as a kind of slavery tending toward death:

> What does all this lead up to? Just because we are not under the law but under grace, are we free to sin? By no means! You must realize that, when you offer yourselves to someone as obedient slaves, you are the slaves of the one you obey, whether yours is the slavery of sin, which leads to death, or of obedience, which leads to justice. Thanks be to God, though once you were slaves of sin, you sincerely obeyed that rule of teaching which was imparted to you; freed from your sin, you became slaves of justice. (I

use the following example from human affairs because of your weak human nature.) Just as formerly you enslaved your bodies to impurity and licentiousness for their degradation, make them now the servants of justice for their sanctification. When you were slaves of sin, you had freedom from justice. What benefit did you then enjoy? Things you are now ashamed of, all of them tending toward death. But now that you are freed from sin and have become slaves of God, your benefit is sanctification as you tend toward eternal life. The wages of sin is death, but the gift of God is eternal life in Christ Jesus our Lord.

Failure to acknowledge the reality of sin is plainly a perilous business. For if we do not acknowledge our sin, we are denying that we have injured ourselves and making impossible the one thing which can repair the damage — a right choice to undo the sinful one.

Even in the best of circumstances, of

course, we can't take the place of God and pardon our own sins. Pardoning sin is something God does, not we. But we do have the ability either to open ourselves to God's pardon or to throw a roadblock in the way. Sorrow for sin is a necessary precondition of God's pardon; and acknowledgment of sin is a necessary precondition of sorrow. The first epistle of Saint John (1:8-9) remarks:

> If we say, "We are free of the guilt of
>   sin,"
> we deceive ourselves. . . .
> But if we acknowledge our sins,
> he who is just can be trusted
> to forgive our sins
> and cleanse us from every wrong.

The distinction between original sin and personal sin is only the first of several distinctions which are necessary for an adequate understanding of sin. Before proceeding further along that line, however, we need to reflect for a while on a still more basic question: what is moral "good" and what is moral "evil"? Having seen the difference, we will then be in a better position to appreciate the differences among various kinds of sins; we'll also have a better grasp of why we need penance and reconciliation.

# CHAPTER 4

# Will Being Good Make Me Happy?

In the sacrament of penance, sins are forgiven. Evidently, then, in order to appreciate penance we must know what sin is and what it does. And to understand the destructive consequences of sin — why, as Saint Paul tells us, "the wages of sin is death" — it is necessary to situate moral evil in the context of a broad overview of the moral life.

Sin offends God. But why is he offended? Is it because sin hurts *him*, takes something away from him? Evidently not. Rather, we can see sin's offense against God in the following terms.

God has a wise and loving plan for us, a plan which he, a true father and friend, wants to see accomplished. But sin departs from this plan for our well-being and fulfillment, and, in doing so, leaves us broken and mutilated instead of whole, healthy, and holy as God wants his children to be. Sin thus ignores and repudiates God's care and love; by sin we treat God as ungrateful children do their parents. It is in this sense that sin offends God.

The "death" to which sin leads is commonly, and correctly, understood by Christians as the loss of eternal happiness and fulfillment in heaven. But the death associated with immorality also begins here and now, with the mutilation of personality that sin entails. Sin is a kind of existential suicide.

We can see why that is so, and why sin has such a pervasive and corrupting effect in individual and social life, by beginning with a very simple question: will being good make me happy?

A lot of us don't like to ask that question. Not out loud anyway. It sounds too selfish to suit our self-image and the image we'd like others to have of us.

But if we are honest, we know that the question does nag us. *Will* being good make me happy? There is plenty of evidence that doing the right thing gets in the way of happiness, while cutting corners can pay off. If so, why try to be good?

One traditional answer, as we have seen, stresses reward and punishment in the afterlife. If you're good, you'll go to heaven; if you're bad, you'll go to hell. While that isn't wrong, it suggests a rather narrow vision of the here and now, implying that in this world "goodness" and "happiness" don't have much connection. As a practical matter, many people find the promise of a payoff later scant inducement to live good lives.

The question also has a better answer, though, one which doesn't conflict with the fact that living a good life will lead to eternal happiness, but which enriches the discussion by showing how goodness and happiness are related in this life as well as the next. The answer nevertheless requires that we be very clear and precise about the meaning of some commonly used (and misused) terms.

To begin with, what do we mean by happiness? People use that one word to express several different ideas.

One meaning is pleasure, and a working definition of pleasure is "a gratifying state of consciousness." People experience pleasure in eating a good meal, having a drink, relaxing in the sun, or engaging in any one of the innumerable other activities which make them feel good.

There's nothing wrong with pleasure. That needs emphasizing because many discussions of these matters seem to share the puritanical assumption that pleasure, if not exactly evil, is at least a little shady — something which *really* good people would try to avoid. The nervous proselytizing of propagandists for the playboy mentality and the visibly driven behavior of practitioners of the philosophy that "you only go around once" suggest that at the back of their minds they also harbor this view, which they must strive mightily to overcome. Puritanism is a long time dying.

At the same time, it's clear that pleasure is too limited to be the most satisfying kind of happiness we can imagine, for pleasure means a gratifying state of consciousness, and people are more than states of consciousness.

You can see that with an example from the realm of science fiction. Suppose a mad scientist learned how to keep a brain alive and fed it nothing but pleasure-producing stimuli. The brain would be experiencing constant pleasure — but nobody would say this kind of existence is what is meant by real human happiness.

People who seek some version of nirvana through drugs, sex, or alcohol are in a comparable situation. In many cases, their behavior proves self-destructive. Even if it doesn't, such one-dimensional pursuit of pleasure is a dead-end detour on the road to authentic happiness, a way of gratifying part of oneself but not the whole self.

Another view identifies happiness with achieving goals and objectives. Study hard and get a diploma. Work hard and get a raise. Exercise hard and get a healthier you.

Again, there is nothing wrong with this. A great deal of our time necessarily is taken up in pursuing goals and objectives. Careful planning, hard work, and efficiency are commendable in this enterprise. There is no merit in daydreaming, laziness, and sloppy performance.

Yet the pursuit of goals, though a necessary part of life, isn't the fullest sort of happiness we can imagine.

For one thing, even when they try their best, people don't always reach their objectives. Students study hard but flunk exams. Workers do a good job but don't get raises. People exercise hard and drop dead of heart attacks. Some happiness!

For another thing, even when we achieve our goals, we're likely to be more or less disappointed. Who hasn't yearned for something (a new car, say), finally gotten it, and found that the satisfaction of having it was fleeting? No sooner do we achieve something than we want something else. Reaching one objective is a starting-point for setting out in restless pursuit of another. If that is the fullest happiness people can enjoy, it leaves a lot to be desired.

But there is a third meaning of happiness which meets our expectations as neither pleasure nor the achieving of limited goals does: it can satisfy us continually, it can satisfy us here and now, and it can satisfy us in all fundamental aspects of our personhood. Its name is fulfillment.

At first, "fulfillment" sounds like a word out of the wonderful world of advertising. Many very limited experiences, from drinking beer to taking a vacation, are said to be fulfilling. But fulfillment also has a more precise sense: participation in human goods.

What exactly does that mean? A case in point may help.

Suppose Joe runs to keep in shape. The happiness it gives him is of the kind described above — doing something to achieve a goal. There is nothing wrong with that, but neither does it involve fulfillment properly so called.

Suppose Jim is also a running enthusiast. Maybe keeping in shape is part of what he has in view. But maybe, too, he runs just because he likes it. In that case, the activity is meaningful for him in its own right at the time he is engaging in it. For Jim, running is a way of participating in a human good — a good which might be called "play." It is the happiness arising from this kind of activity, performed for its own sake in order to participate here and now in a human good, which is "fulfillment" in its precise sense.

This fulfillment is moreover not a merely individualistic thing. Although it will often not be uppermost in our minds, moral goodness always requires that we choose and act not just for our own sakes but for the fulfillment of the other members of the human community. A morally good person is more concerned that the good be realized — even by other members of the community — than that he or she realize it.

When what we do is fulfilling, we are shaping ourselves as persons, for the human goods in which we participate are aspects of our personhood. One list identifies eight basic human goods — life, play, aesthetic experience, speculative knowledge, integrity, practical reasonableness or authenticity, friendship, and religion — though obviously there are many others, which are aspects or combinations of these.

However we enumerate and name them, fundamental goods of this sort are not abstractions. They are aspects of human personhood. They tell us what we and other people are or can be.

No one, of course, can be or do everything at the same time and to the same extent. Quite appropriately, one individual places the emphasis on the scholarly pursuit of knowledge, another on the cultivation of interpersonal relationships, a third on the nurturing of life (for example, through the practice of parenthood or the healing arts). But at least every individual can and should refrain from *acting against* any basic human purpose. For that is what immorality — sin — means. The essence of sin is a choice against one (or more) of the fundamental goods of the human person.

This suggests why being good involves more than just living by external rules, and why being bad (committing sin) involves more than violating them. To suppose otherwise is to externalize morality — to reduce goodness to obeying a set of rules imposed from outside. That is legalism, a view of morality shared as often by proponents of the "new morality" as by supporters of the "old."

In place of legalism, it is important to see the intrinsic link between morality and personhood: human goods tell us what we and other persons are or can be; respect for these goods is essential to morality; and the morally good individual therefore is fulfilled precisely by being open to all the possibilities of personhood.

Much of what has been said up to now can be expressed in specifically Christian terms by speaking of charity — that is, love of God and neighbor. Thus, love of God consists in conformity to his good will for the integrity of creation and redemption, and specifically for our fulfillment and the fulfillment of the human community. Love of neighbor consists in willing the fulfillment of others in respect to all the goods of the human person, in communion with God, in which we also hope to be included.

What then keeps me from being happy in the full and authentic sense in which we've defined happiness? The answer should be apparent.

The obstacles to happiness are whatever blocks fulfillment — and fulfillment comes through respecting and participating in human goods, which together add up to a kind of outline of what people are capable of being.

Even the happiness of heaven won't be a sharp break from this pattern. In heaven we will enjoy the fullest possible realization of our personhood. Fulfillment won't mean putting aside our humanity but realizing it to the utmost through fulfillment in Christ.

"All very nice," someone might reply,

"but such lofty talk doesn't say much. As a practical matter, *how* is a person supposed to translate abstractions like these into concrete terms in everyday life? How are people supposed to be 'fulfilled' while coping with the pressures of family life, the demands of humdrum work, the countless challenges involved in getting through a day?"

It is literally a matter of choice. Whether or not we know fulfillment depends on how we choose. Fulfillment is within our grasp if we learn to choose rightly and do so consistently. If not, sooner or later our efforts to be happy will come to grief. Hence the problem with any approach which either denies the reality of free choice or advocates ways of choosing which prevent fulfillment.

Determinism denies that there is such a thing as free choice. Some philosophers hold deterministic theories, and determinism is also influential in psychology and the social sciences. That's not to say there is anything wrong with philosophy, psychology, and the social sciences as such. But it is important to be aware of the deterministic underpinnings of some theories which are operative in these fields.

Whatever the specifics of any particular theory may be, determinism comes down to saying that we don't really choose freely. Instead, our decisions are programmed for us in advance by heredity, by environment (the way we were brought up and the circumstances in which we live), or by some combination of the two.

That isn't entirely wrong. Heredity and environment do have a powerful impact on our ability to make free choices. For one thing, they cut down the number of options from among which we can choose. Herman, five foot two, doesn't have the option of being a professional basketball player. Ethel, a file clerk making ten thousand a year, doesn't have the option of joining a country club. And so on.

For another thing, cultural and psychological factors limit our capacity for free choice. People often act on the basis of drives and compulsions of which they are scarcely aware and over which they have little control. In that sense, we may all be "unfree" to some degree in some areas of our lives.

Yet we do have the experience of choosing freely. We recognize it when we confront two or more options — say, to read a good book or go to a concert — and are undecided between them. The indecision itself is a sign of freedom. Nothing is forcing us in one direction or another. We have to make up our minds; we have to choose.

Determinists dismiss that type of experience (the experience of choosing freely) as an illusion, but they have no valid reasons for doing so. Arguments for determinism can't avoid assuming that in at least one matter we *are* free: free enough to follow the argument that determinism is true. Thus determinism refutes itself as a theoretical explanation of human behavior. But a self-refuting theory provides no grounds for dismissing as an illusion the common experience that, at least some times and in some matters, we are indeed free to choose as we will.

To make good use of freedom, then, it is essential that we first of all recognize that it exists. It is also essential that we learn *how* to use it in a way which contributes to our fulfillment.

Will being good make me happy? Where fulfillment is at issue, it is the only way.

But that doesn't mean it will come cheaply.

Happiness of this kind isn't easy. It is often simpler to settle for the limited happiness associated with pleasure or achieving specific goals. It is often more convenient to turn against a human good in order to get out of a tight spot (for instance, solving a problem by cheating on an exam, by telling a lie, or by having an abortion). It is convenient, in other words, to sin. But in doing so, people aren't just breaking rules — they are closing off, to a greater or lesser degree, avenues for realizing the capacities of their personhood. And that is a kind of existential suicide. Saint Paul, it seems, was correct in telling us: "The wages of sin is death."

# CHAPTER 5

# *The Role of Choice*

As a result of original sin, we — by ourselves — are literally powerless to live good lives. Yet we still have our freedom. God, moreover, does not abandon anyone who is willing to accept his help. And so, God helping, *we* — ourselves, with the Holy Spirit — can choose rightly and in doing so can live good, holy lives. To sin, by contrast, means choosing wrongly — not just making mistaken choices but choosing in a way which is morally wrong. Continuing our consideration of the moral context of the sacrament of penance, we need now to reflect on the crucial role of choice and especially on *how* to choose.

There are in fact theories which make the task more difficult than it needs to be. Among the most troublesome, because of its apparent plausibility, is the idea that moral goodness lies in choosing whatever will produce the greater good and the least harm.

What on earth, someone might say, is wrong with that? Surely nobody would argue that goodness lies in choices which produce the *least* good or the *most* harm. But that is not the point. The point instead is that the notion of choosing by the formula of the "greatest good" and the "least harm" rests on a false assumption which leads to disastrous confusion about how to choose well.

The essence of choosing well lies in respecting all the goods of the human person in oneself and others. It isn't possible to choose all the goods simultaneously, but it is possible to choose in such a way that one does not close oneself to any good in the act of choosing. By contrast, the "greatest good, least harm" approach makes this inevitable.

That needs explaining.

Suppose Major Jones wants information about the disposition of enemy troops facing his men in battle. Some prisoners have just been brought to his headquarters. To find out what he needs to know, he orders them tortured to death, one at a time, until one finally cracks. He reasons that a few lives will be lost that way, but many other lives will be saved.

Suppose Mrs. Smith, a married woman with several children, finds herself unexpectedly pregnant again. As matters stand, the family is just making it financially. Another baby will strain economic resources to the breaking point. Reluctantly, the Smiths opt for abortion. They reason that it is in the best interests of the family as a whole.

In both cases — and in many similar though less dramatic ones — the idea of the "greatest good" underlies the choice which is made. Take some lives in order to save other lives. Destroy an unborn life in order to make things easier for persons who've been born. The principle of such choices is quantitative. Numbers count.

But in such cases the human good of some persons is sacrificed to the human good of others. Despite the praiseworthy ends they may have in view, people who choose in this way are willing to act — and *do* act — against human goods. The "greatest good" formula leads to the conclusion that the end justifies the means.

Furthermore, neat and precise as it sounds, the formula is in fact unworkable. There are several reasons.

First, it assumes that we can know and take into account all the consequences of our actions for all the persons they will affect. But we can't. Instead we limit our vision — to a certain period of time, a certain group of persons, certain immediate consequences — while excluding what we can't foresee so well or aren't so interested in.

One argument for dropping the atomic bomb on Hiroshima and Nagasaki, for example, is that doing so cut short — as it was meant to do — World War II and consequently saved many lives. That may very well be true. But how do the development and use of the bomb look in the light of what has happened since 1945? Is the world a happier, safer place? Even someone who can accept the killing of noncombatants by terror-bombing on the grounds that this hastened the end of the war has difficulty arguing that the results of opening the nuclear Pandora's box — a prolonged arms race raising the specter of nuclear holocaust on a scale far vaster than Hiroshima and Nagasaki — have been desirable.

Second, human goods themselves can't be weighed and measured as the calculation of the "greatest good" requires. How to compare, say, the value of "life" and the value of "truth"? What is the common denominator — the scale on which one outweighs the other? There is no such scale.

Basic human goods are not reducible to some ultrafundamental "good" underlying all of them, nor are they reducible to one another. Each basic good of the human person is fundamental and inviolable. If the reverse is true — if the goods of persons may be violated for the sake of some "greater good" — ideas like the sanctity of life and the dignity and rights of human persons are meaningless. No human good, and indeed no human person, is safe from the calculus that violating the good in a particular instance serves a greater good.

All this may seem to have strayed a long way from the question of happiness. But it lies at the heart of that matter, as well as at the heart of what constitutes a sinful choice.

As we have seen, happiness has several different meanings. Pleasure and the achieving of limited goals and objectives are among these. There is nothing wrong with pleasure, nor is there anything wrong with pursuing and achieving goals. But they can raise a problem.

People who suppose that the fullest happiness of which human beings are capable is either pleasure or the achievement of limited goals are vulnerable to the notion that it is morally acceptable to sacrifice human goods — and therefore human persons — in order to get the gratification or success they want. This willingness to choose against the good of the human person is the essence of a sinful choice.

There is, however, another meaning of happiness: fulfillment. This is the happiness which comes from participating in human goods. To be sure, no one can participate in all these goods simultaneously and to the same degree. But all of us *can* remain open in our choices to all of the goods: we can refrain from choosing and acting against any good of the human person either in ourselves or in others. This is the minimal requirement for moral goodness and fulfillment. As such, it is central and indispensable to happiness.

* * *

Moral goodness and human fulfillment intersect. The crossroads at which they converge is free choice.

The choices we make are crucial both to our moral lives and our happiness. In both respects, however, the issue isn't so much *what* we choose as *how* we choose. The possibilities for choice are almost without number, but the ways of choosing are only two.

The matter may be large or it may be small, but in either case choosing badly — sinning — expresses a will to damage or impede the good in ourselves or others. This brings about a real change in our moral identities: we make ourselves persons who are willing to act against human goods. People who will to lie (choose against truth) make themselves liars. People who will to steal (choose against justice) make themselves thieves. People who will to kill (choose against life) make themselves murderers.

Even small choices are important to the extent that they are acts of self-determination. Choosing badly in small matters paves the way to choosing badly in large matters — not because a moral domino theory decrees it, but because choices form our moral identities and set the stage for more choices of the same sort.

This is especially true of the kind of choice called "commitment." Commitments are, as it were, "umbrella" choices which, once made, require subsequent implementing choices. Commitments may involve large matters or small, but they always have a particular importance inasmuch as they pave the way to — indeed, demand — additional choices.

For its part, choosing well means choosing a human good in a way that leaves one open to *all* the goods of the human person. The contrast between choosing well and choosing badly is striking, both in the way the choice is made and in its psychological manifestations. Let's see what that means in the case of a commitment involving, in its own right, fairly small matters.

Meet Fred. Life's getting complicated for him. He's recently been elected to the parish council, but he's also a member of a bowling team and lately has been taking a course in art appreciation at the local community college. There are just so many days in a week. Something has to give.

Fred thinks it over. At first the choice isn't easy. He finds rewards in all the activities he's involved in. But finally he decides. He'll stay with the parish council but drop the bowling team and the art appreciation course. He reasons this way:

"Bowling doesn't turn me on any more, and I'm getting bored with the other guys on the team. Rolling a ball at some sticks of wood is a pretty dumb way to spend your time anyhow. The same is true of art appreciation. I don't know why I'm hanging around with a bunch of frustrated Rembrandts.

"But the parish council — that's a different story. Other people look up to me, and I can see the pastor takes what I say seriously. High time I got some recognition around here! And I don't mind doing the parish a good turn either."

Fred has chosen badly — not because staying on the parish council is wrong, any more than either of the other two options would be wrong. Nor has he chosen badly because budgeting his time is wrong (as a matter of fact, it's the sensible thing to do in the circumstances), but because in the act of choosing he belittled the goods embodied in the bowling team and the art class.

Before choosing, Fred is open to the good in all three options. He is right to be open, for there *is* good there — service to religion in the parish council, recreation in the bowling team, aesthetic appreciation in the art class, and probably friendship in all three. Furthermore, these goods aren't abstractions; they correspond to aspects of Fred's personhood into which he breathes life by choosing them.

In making his decision, however, Fred sets his will against some of these goods. Thus he turns against elements of his personhood. The problem isn't that he gives up a bowling team and an art appreciation course; it's that he denies that they represent anything worthwhile and so repudiates something in himself which previously sought and found fulfillment.

Lest there be any confusion, I'm not suggesting that Fred has committed a serious sin. What's at stake is too small for that. But I *am* noting that the pattern of choosing present here repeats itself consistently in much larger decisions which may indeed be gravely sinful. To that extent, in choosing this way Fred *may* be setting himself up — even in this trivial instance — for a really serious fall on another occasion.

The difficulty is apparent from the way Fred verbalizes his choice. The old expression "cutting off your nose to spite your face" comes to mind — but in this case the "cutting off" has taken place at a level of the personality much deeper than a nose.

Yet Fred doesn't have to choose like this. Instead he can choose in a way that leaves him open to the goods which are present in all the options. True, some things *can't* be chosen well precisely because choosing them unavoidably involves setting one's will against human goods. (That would be the case, for instance, if Fred decided to spend his spare time peddling drugs.) But this isn't Fred's situation, and so it is possible for him to choose well among all of the options he actually faces. In that case, he might express his choice as follows:

"I like the fellows on the bowling team, and I enjoy the game itself, but I can always go back to it later. Same thing with art appreciation. It's a lot of fun, and you meet some interesting people. I don't have to do it right now though.

"I've been elected to a term on the parish council, and I think I owe it to the others to give it a good shot. I'm glad of this opportunity to work with a fine bunch of people and do something for the parish, and for now at least that's where I'd better put the emphasis."

In other words: bowling is good and art appreciation is good, but nobody can do everything simultaneously. Fred has made his choice while remaining open to the good which is present in the options he didn't choose. He has chosen well.

As noted, the choices called commitments are particularly important to the whole process of choosing. Many are of a vocational nature. There are small commitments (membership on a bowling team or a parish council, for instance) and large ones (such as the choice of marriage or the priesthood or religious life), but all are alike in this — they set the stage for many subsequent choices. In this way they provide the framework for our moral lives and our fulfillment as persons.

It is important to make commitments as consciously and responsibly as possible. Sometimes people drift into extremely large commitments, including immoral ones, carelessly and without much attention. When they wake up to their situation, it may be too late to do much about it without a great deal of suffering for themselves and others.

Similarly, it is important to make commitments that mesh well. A person who is overcommitted — involved in too many things to do justice to any — may mean well but is guilty of a fault.

At the same time, nobody knows in undertaking a very large commitment, especially one of a vocational nature, what living it out will entail. For such a commitment, like that to marriage, is not the end of moral creativity but its beginning. Over a period of time the choices demanded of us in living up to our serious commitments require the very best we're capable of and shape us profoundly as persons.

When a couple marry, for instance, they realize (unless they are exceptionally featherbrained) that living out their commitment

69

will demand much of them — fidelity, patience, generosity, and a lot else. But what will fidelity, patience, generosity, and the rest mean in practice for them in the years ahead? What specific choices will they have to make to honor their commitment? That is something they will only learn by living out the commitment. Doing so will be their path to fulfillment, beginning in this life and culminating in the next.

Many commitments have a strong social dimension. Through them we "build community," as the current jargon puts it. What this means is that people come together in a true moral unity for the sake of particular purposes or goods which they seek to realize in common. A family is a simple example of community in this sense; the Church is a large and complex one.

Community, too, is extremely important to our moral lives and fulfillment. Commitment to healthy communities pursuing appropriate purposes in legitimate ways is enriching, while commitment to communities organized for harmful purposes — a gang of criminals, for instance — is destructive.

Moreover, community enables us to

compensate for our individual limitations. No one can realize all the goods or purposes of human beings in one's own life, but sharing in the life of a community makes it possible for each member to share to some degree in goods beyond one's reach as an individual. For people with "community spirit" in a large and generous sense, it is more important that the good be realized than that they realize it individualistically.

The fullest happiness of which human beings are capable is fulfillment — participation in the goods which together make up a kind of outline of human possibilities. Fulfillment depends on how we choose: in a way that tends to close us off to goods we don't opt for here and now, or in a way that leaves us open to the full and dazzling range of human purposes. Commitment and community are central to this process. Combining all these elements as they should be combined is the key to moral goodness and to happiness.

But such happiness by no means comes cheap. Refusing to turn against any of the goods in our choices can involve us in real, finite suffering. There are powerful inducements to avoid suffering and take the easy route to gratification by setting the will against one good of the human person for the sake of another. For all of us, sin is a real possibility at every moment. We need the sacrament of penance — for pardon when we do choose badly and for help in choosing well.

# CHAPTER 6

# Conscience

Sin and morality aren't the only matters about which there is confusion today. For many people, one of the biggest sources of uncertainty is conscience. False ideas about conscience — its nature and its role — have probably contributed to the current decline in confession. What, then, *is* this thing we call conscience?

A lot of people aren't too sure. Persons influenced by Freudian psychology tend to confuse conscience with what that system calls superego — the guilt-ridden, more or less neurotic residue of commands and prohibitions imposed by authority figures in early childhood. In fact, however, superego can be an obstacle to the functioning of authentic conscience, substituting feelings of guilt and anxiety for clear, rational judgments of right and wrong. (This, it seems, is at least part of the explanation for the familiar confession-related problem of scrupulosity.) Superego and conscience are not the same thing.

Others think of conscience as a mysterious voice whispering in their ears and telling them what to do and not to do. I, however, have never heard that voice, and I suspect most people haven't. Still others, for all practical purposes, equate conscience with the laws and rules and social conventions of the particular groups with which they identify — laws, rules, and conventions which they may not always observe, but which they nevertheless take to be normative. Such regulations are, however, evidently *external* to us — they come to us from outside — and conscience, whatever it may be, is something within.

So — to repeat — what is conscience?

In the Catholic tradition there is an enormous literature on the subject, and even in that body of literature "conscience" is used in several different senses. For present purposes, though, it's best to give the word the meaning which many of us learned in school: conscience is our last, best practical judgment that here and now some proposed course of action is or isn't morally right.

This is the sense in which Thomas Aquinas used the term, and it is also the key meaning of "conscience" as it is used by the Second Vatican Council.

The exercise or use of conscience in this sense is a fully personal act. Germain Grisez, a distinguished American theologian and philosopher, puts it like this:

> Judgments of right and wrong by a person with a mature conscience express more than early training or awareness of what is socially required. They say what ought to be required, what one will require of oneself if one is reasonable. To think of morality as an area in which one is made to feel guilty or as a set of rules which someone else imposes, expresses an immature conscience. By contrast, a person of mature conscience thinks of morality as a matter of real human goodness and reasonableness. For such a person, to do what is wrong is a kind of self-mutilation.

When conscience is thought of in this way, it is self-evident that a person ought to follow conscience. Unfortunately, quite a few people get no further than that. Thus one often hears people say that in acting in such-and-such a way, they are "doing what their conscience tells them is right."

That's fine as far as it goes, but there is another step that is important to take: namely, is what their consciences are telling them right, *really* right? Does it conform to the objective norms of morality? Unless one is willing to examine this question seriously and carefully, "following conscience" tends to become an exercise in mere arbitrariness, by which a person acts on impulse and whim. This in fact can be sinful in itself.

It is true that a person is obliged to "follow conscience" even when his or her conscience is mistaken. But the fact that an individual is following conscience in such cases does not absolve him of all responsibility. If the error, the mistake in judgment, is his own fault, he is responsible for the wrong he does in following a mistaken conscience. The Second Vatican Council sketched out the relevant distinctions in these two sentences: "Yet it often happens that conscience goes astray through ignorance which it is unable to avoid, without thereby losing its dignity. This cannot be said of the man who takes little trouble to find out what is true and good, or when conscience is by degrees almost blinded through the habit of committing sin" (*Church in the Modern World*, 16).

Where does conscience get its norms, the bases for its judgments of right and wrong? A primary source is what has traditionally been called "natural law."

In his letter to the Romans, Saint Paul (without of course using terminology which only was developed much later) speaks at length of the law of reason — the natural moral law — implanted in the hearts of all human beings, Gentiles just as much as Jews. He argues that people *can* know this law, that they *ought* to know it and observe it, and that they will rightly be judged according to whether they do or do not. He conceives of conscience as the faculty by which judgments of right and wrong based on this natural moral law are made. Thus, in Romans 2:12-16, he writes:

Sinners who do not have the law [here Paul means the Mosaic law revealed to the Jewish people by God] will perish without reference to it; sinners bound by the law will be judged in accordance with it. For it is not those who hear the law who are just in the sight of God; it is those who keep it who will be declared just. When Gentiles who do not have the law keep it as by instinct [now Paul is starting to speak of the natural moral law], these men although without the law serve as a law for themselves. They show that the demands of the law are written in their hearts. Their conscience bears witness together with that law, and their thoughts will accuse or defend them on the day when, in accordance with the gospel I preach, God will pass judgment on the secrets of men through Christ Jesus.

It should be clear from what's been said so far that our first responsibility, as far as conscience is concerned, is to form our consciences correctly so that our moral judgments will not only be "conscientious" or "sincere" but true. And, without going into excessive detail, it can be said that, in general, conscience formation involves study and reflection in three specific areas.

First, the principles of the moral law (what has traditionally been called the natural law). Second, the exploration of practical possibilities. This is important because people often say in effect, "I see no way out of this situation except to do 'X' " — when "X" is something which is morally wrong. In fact, there is always a way out that does not involve doing moral evil; but many people are so conditioned that they simply cannot see the morally correct alternative if it involves some inconvenience or pain for them. Third, the application of moral principles to the facts of the case — both new situations which we are confronting for the first time, and also existing situations whose moral appropriateness we are reviewing.

Where, a Catholic reader may ask, does the Church fit into this scheme of things?

Since I am not writing a book about the Catholic Church and its special claims as a teacher, I am not going to try to "prove" anything in particular about the Church. Rather, I take certain things for granted, as I assume most other Catholics more or less do, even in these confused times. My assumptions include the following:

First, that there is a great deal of moral truth which, at least in principle, we are capable of knowing on our own, without the help of the Church. In general, this body of moral truth corresponds to the content of natural law.

Second, that although we *can* know this body of moral truth on our own, very often we do not. Confusion, lack of time, our sinful inclinations, and other factors account for that.

Third, that there are also a number of important truths pertaining to morality which we *cannot* expect to know apart from revelation.

And, finally, that the functioning of the Church as a teacher of moral truth is absolutely necessary with regard to the truths which we can't know apart from revelation and necessary as a practical matter with regard to many truths of the natural moral law which we could — but generally don't — arrive at on our own.

The Second Vatican Council expresses all this by saying: "The Catholic Church is by the will of Christ the teacher of truth. It is her duty to proclaim and teach with authority the truth which is Christ and, at the same time, to declare and confirm by her authority the principles of the moral order which spring from human nature itself" (*Religious Liberty*, 14).

By no means, however, does this mean that the Catholic conscience exists in passive and slavish dependence on the Church. The moral teaching of the Church does bind persons: acceptance of the Church and its teaching follows from the act of faith, itself a free commitment which one ought to make because one sees the goodness of doing so; furthermore, loyal Catholics who comprehend the Church's divinely given role as a teacher of moral truth will accept and obey its teaching on those grounds also. But this still leaves a vast field where initiative and moral creativity are required.

Specifically, it is up to us to discern, in light of our personal vocations and commitments, our *positive* obligations in fulfilling moral precepts — what we *should* do rather than what we should not. The conscience of an informed and loyal Catholic has much work to do in carrying out this complex but rewarding task.

* * *

So far we have looked at several general notions — evil, sin (original and personal), happiness and morality, conscience. To see where the sacrament of penance fits in, it is now necessary to become more specific. I'll begin by taking up an old but valid distinction — that between mortal sin and venial sin.

# CHAPTER 7

# Mortal Sin, Venial Sin, Social Sin

In recent years there has been a tendency to look upon mortal sin as if it were the Loch Ness monster of morality: if it exists at all, its appearances are mighty rare and have little or no personal relevance for most people. But is that really the case? The evidence of Scripture and the teaching of the Church suggest otherwise.

The Old and New Testaments speak often of moral offenses which are so serious that, unless and until repented, they cut off those who commit them from a living relationship with God. Jesus warns in a number of places that this is a real possibility.

Thus: "Once there was a rich man who dressed in purple and linen and feasted splendidly every day. At his gate lay a beggar named Lazarus who was covered with sores. Lazarus longed to eat the scraps that fell from the rich man's table. The dogs even came and licked his sores. Eventually the beggar died. He was carried by angels to the bosom of Abraham. The rich man likewise died and was buried. From the abode of the dead where he was in torment, he raised his eyes and saw Abraham afar off, and Lazarus resting in his bosom" (Luke 16:19-23).

The rich man asks for relief; Abraham tells him none is possible. Then the unfortunate man begs another favor: send Lazarus to the home of his five brothers as a warning so that they will not suffer the same unhappy fate. Impossible, says Abraham again. "If they do not listen to Moses and the prophets" — that is, if they do not heed God's teaching already amply available to them — "they will not be convinced even if one should rise from the dead" (Luke 16:31). This is not a parable to inspire complacency among followers of the risen Jesus on the subject of mortal sin and its consequences.

The theological and pastoral tradition of the Church identifies three elements as essential to mortal sin: grave matter (and "matter" of some kinds is always, intrinsically "grave"), full knowledge, and deliberate consent.

To say this, of course, is to repeat the old catechism definition of mortal sin. But the old catechism was simply reflecting what Pope John Paul II calls a "painful experience" shared by many people — namely, "that by a conscious and free act of their wills they can change course and go in a direction opposed to God's will, separating themselves from God, rejecting loving communion with him, detaching themselves from the life-principle which God is, and consequently choosing death."

Is this an extremely rare occurrence? The question, evidently, is one which each individual must answer for himself, but the answer shouldn't be given on the basis of blithe confidence that it's virtually impossible to sin mortally.

Of late it has sometimes been suggested that sins should be divided into three categories instead of the traditional two. The categories proposed are "venial," "grave," and "mortal," and the implication is that, although the last kind — mortal sin — is very bad, it isn't something most of us are likely ever to commit.

In practical terms, mortal sin is presented as a turning-away from God which amounts to personal and express hatred. It is as if an individual were not only to say no to God, but to spend a lifetime shouting no, over and over again, up to and through the very moment of death itself.

This view of mortal sin is related to some versions of what theologians call "fundamental option" theory. They hold that fundamental option is a kind of choice but not an ordinary one. It is the total orientation of the self toward God or away from God. Understood this way, "fundamental option" can be very comforting. For who in his right mind would choose to orient himself fundamentally and radically *away* from God? And if anyone did so, wouldn't that be evidence in itself that he wasn't in his "right" mind, and therefore couldn't be held accountable?

"True," I may say, "in the course of a lifetime I am likely to commit a few peccadillos — a little hatred here, a bit of lust there, a certain amount of dishonesty I'd rather other people didn't know about. But it's not as if these things changed my fundamental option. For basically, you see, I'd still rather be 'for' God than 'against' him, since the consequences of being against God could be unpleasant."

Fundamental-option theories can't be dismissed out of hand, but neither can everything that goes by the name of "fundamental option" be accepted. The account just given may represent a rather simplistic version, but it's not so far removed from the way some people think. For a better understanding of fundamental option, it's necessary first to see what the "fundamental option" of Christian life really is.

In fact, the fundamental Christian option is the act of living faith — commitment to Jesus Christ, determination to cultivate a personal relationship with him, and consistent striving to choose and act in light of this. Considered in this way, it is clear that, as the Holy Father says, "the fundamental orientation can be radically changed by individual acts." In other words, some choices — in this case, mortal sins — are so inimical to our relationship with Christ, so opposed to behavior consistent with that relationship, that the relationship itself is disrupted unless and until we mend our ways.

We see this clearly enough in our other

relationships. There is, for example, no realistic sense in which I can call myself the "friend" of a person toward whom here and now I am performing a profoundly hostile action. To call myself the friend of someone whom I am deeply offending at this moment makes a mockery of language and good sense. In much the same way, it is pointless to pretend that my relationship with Jesus remains that of friendship when I am deliberately acting contrary to his will in a serious matter. We can take Jesus' word for it:

> He who obeys the commandments he
>     has from me
> is the man who loves me;. . .
> He who does not love me does not
>     keep my words.
> — John 14:21, 24

It isn't necessary here to provide a lengthy catalogue of mortal sins. As a practical matter, a Catholic is safe in the knowledge that deeds traditionally identified by the Church as constituting the "matter" of grave sins do just that. The deliberate free choice to commit such an action is a mortal sin, which betrays one's living relationship with God unless and until it is repented, (ordinarily) confessed, and forgiven.

Venial sin, by contrast with mortal sin, is a less serious immorality, which does not deprive us of sanctifying grace and sever the living relationship between us and God. This, however, is by no means an argument for complacency about venial sin, expressed in the notion that "it doesn't matter — it's *only* a venial sin."

Two considerations caution us against adopting such an attitude. One is — or should be — our desire for friendship with God. Obviously, there is something lacking in a friendship in which one party frequently and deliberately fails to please the other in small matters, reasoning, "He's willing to put up with it." The other is that, in various ways, venial sin leads to mortal sin. Not that over a period of time the accumulation of venial sins amounts to a sum equal to mortal sin; the point, rather, is that in ways subtle and not so subtle, repeated venial sin undermines our psychological and spiritual defenses, accustoms us to the idea of doing what is wrong as a more or less routine thing, opens us to temptations we'd otherwise not experience, and thus paves the way to mortal sin. Deliberate venial sin should in fact be taken very seriously indeed.

\* \* \*

Lately, as we have seen, another distinction has also become crucial in regard to sin. It is the distinction between personal sin on the one hand and social sin on the other.

The subject of "social sin" is of enormous importance — both in its own right and also, unfortunately, because it generates a great deal of confusion. Social sin has always been a reality of life, but only in recent years has it come to receive much attention in popular preaching and teaching. The result, it appears, is not just a healthy new emphasis on the social dimensions of morality — it is also, apparently, an *un*-healthy *over*-emphasis which in its most extreme forms seems to suggest that the *only* kind of sin, or at least the only kind worth taking seriously, is "social" sin.

"Social sin" has various meanings. One might, for instance, speak of sins relating to social issues — harboring racist attitudes, say, or supporting abortion — as "social" sins. Not only is there nothing wrong with this way of speaking, the emphasis on our obligations (and sins) in the area of social justice is healthy and commendable.

However, "social sin" can also refer to something different: to unjust systems, "structures," and policies which result from and embody sin, and tend to give encouragement to sin. Thus, one might speak of *apartheid* or the legalization of abortion as social sin in this sense.

There is no problem with this second meaning of "social sin" either, provided it doesn't cause us to lose sight of the reality of personal sin. But that can happen — for example, by placing so much emphasis on unjust social "systems" and "structures" that we no longer attach much importance to the evil of our individual, less dramatic acts of infidelity and meanness, or by overlooking the role which our personal sins play in creating and sustaining the situations of "social sin" which we say we deplore. Pope John Paul places particular emphasis on such confusions, speaking of "the watering down and almost the abolition of personal

91

sin, with the recognition only of social guilt and responsibilities."

Actually, as the pope points out, such an attitude has an unintended result: it sharply reduces our capacity for correcting situations of social sin themselves, for "cases of social sin are the result of the accumulation and concentration of many personal sins." The sinful choices and deeds of individuals bring unjust structures and systems into existence and now sustain them in all their oppressive reality.

It is of course possible simply to replace one "system" or "structure" with another; but without a change of heart on the part of individuals, chances are good that the new system will be — or in time will become — as unjust and oppressive as the old. The pattern is cyclical, depressingly repetitive. Only by rooting out the sin in individual human hearts — only, in other words, by conversion — is lasting change for the better ensured.

The difference, and also the link, between personal sin and social sin was one of the major topics on the minds of the bishops attending the 1983 international synod in

Rome. After considerable "to-ing and fro-ing," they came to the unremarkable conclusion that there is a connection — a "nexus" — between the two realities, as well as between personal reconciliation and social reconciliation. Although the point was worth making, it hardly comes as a surprise.

True, there was a tendency in some of the rhetoric to suggest that individual reconciliation leads directly to social reconciliation (there *is* a link, but it is by no means as simple and direct as that). Otherwise, the synod said little except that, other things being equal, Catholics who receive the sacrament of penance sincerely and regularly are probably somewhat less likely to contribute to the proliferation of social evils, and somewhat more likely to work for the eradication of those which already exist, than Catholics who do not.

Laying aside rhetoric, Cardinal Roger Etchegaray, then of Marseilles and now a Vatican official, spoke candidly in reply to a question at a news conference during the synod. The Church, he said, has no "magical solutions" to social problems; its most useful contribution is simply to emphasize —

and to keep on emphasizing in the face of assertions to the contrary — the fact of individual human freedom and moral responsibility.

# CHAPTER 8

# Problems with Confession

Evidently there are many reasons for the decline in reception of the sacrament of penance. One set of reasons, as we have seen, arises from confusion about sin. This confusion is unlikely to be resolved apart from resolving what Bishop Austin Vaughan, auxiliary bishop of New York and a participant in the 1983 synod, called "the pastoral problem: Is mortal sin a daily danger for many of our people, or something very rare, or something in between?"

As a practical matter, many Catholics today apparently just don't think they do anything seriously enough wrong to require them to go out of their way to ask God's pardon. If they're right, we are living in the most blessed era in two millennia of Christian history — a time when the majority of Catholics have already achieved sanctity. If they're wrong, it would appear that quite a few people have a major problem on their hands without realizing it, or at least without admitting it.

Another set of causes for the decline in reception of penance evidently has to do with attitudes toward the sacrament itself. How necessary is it for the forgiveness of sins? Sin aside, how much spiritual benefit does it offer? And aren't there other, better ways of celebrating the sacrament than the one-on-one individual confession which, it appears, some people find distasteful?

Sins — even mortal sins — *can* be forgiven apart from actual reception of the sacrament. (Even so, theologians say that pardon and grace come to the repentant sinner in such a case *through* the sacrament, since it is the definitive means instituted by Christ for the forgiveness of sin. It would take us too far afield trying to understand how that is so, but it does suggest the enormous importance of these gifts, the sacraments, given us by Christ.) In any case, actual reception of penance is the surest way of receiving God's pardon and, considering that the sacrament was instituted by Christ, it is also meant to be the ordinary way.

Thus, Pope John Paul observes, "It would . . . be foolish, as well as presumptuous, to wish arbitrarily to disregard the means of grace and salvation which the Lord has provided and . . . to claim to receive forgiveness while doing without the sacrament which was instituted by Christ precisely for forgiveness."

Another pastoral difficulty which has apparently played a significant part in the decline in confessions in recent years is the problem of bad conscience. A significant number of Catholics have rationalized behavior contrary to the Church's teaching on various matters, especially, it seems, matters of sexual morality; at the same time, they remain more or less uneasy about the rationalization and the behavior. The rationalization makes it impossible for them to mention the behavior in confession, while the uneasiness makes it difficult for them *not* to mention it. For many, it seems, the solution is to stay away from confession, and then to rationalize *that* on various grounds.

Perhaps there's a connection here with another phenomenon of contemporary Catholic life in the United States. Not many people go to confession regularly and frequently, yet at most Masses today virtually everyone comes forward to receive Holy Communion. This is a sensitive subject; no one can pronounce definitively on another's interior fitness for Communion. But the conjunction of the two things — infrequent confession, frequent Communion — at least suggests a decline in sensitivity toward the Blessed Sacrament. Yes, Christ *does* want us to receive him frequently in this sacrament. But to do so worthily, we must first meet some basic conditions — notably, that we be in the state of grace — or else this encounter itself can become a serious abuse of a great privilege.

This overall state of affairs seems also to constitute part of the explanation for the current interest in expanding the practice of general absolution.

The Church permits general absolution — absolution granted to a group of penitents without the immediate individual confession of sins — in exceptional circumstances of urgent, unforeseen necessity (the classic cases cited are wartime situations and disasters). Even so, persons who receive general absolution in this way should individually confess their mortal sins, if any, at the earliest opportunity. This is required not only by canon law but by the nature of the sacrament itself.

Where, by abuse, the practice of general absolution has become more or less common, it seems likely that another abuse accompanies it: ignoring the requirement of individual confession of serious sin. In such circumstances, absolution without confession can confer on the sinner a subjective *experience* of reconciliation — a *feeling* of being forgiven — without the need to confront and reject his or her specific sinfulness. To that extent, it "solves" the problem of bad conscience, but at what cost to the integrity and spiritual health of the persons involved, only God can say.

"A conscience which remains silent is a sick conscience," writes Cardinal Joseph Ratzinger, the theologian who heads the Vatican's Congregation for the Doctrine of the Faith. "A man unable to recognize his guilt and who continues to suffer from it is not a liberated man, but a spiritual cripple." This precisely is the danger posed by general absolution without the individual confession of sins.

And yet — "Why bother?" some people ask about individual confession. "Confession is an irksome and distasteful thing. Why can't I just be absolved with a group and let it go at that?"

Pope John Paul's answer emphasizes the personal character of sin and, appropriately, the personal character of the forgiveness of sin through confession and sacramental reconciliation. "Nothing," he writes, "is more personal and intimate than this sacrament, in which the sinner stands alone before God with his sin, repentance, and trust. No one can repent in his place or ask forgiveness of his sin. . . . Everything takes place between the individual alone and God."

Reflecting on these words, Cardinal Joseph Bernardin of Chicago, another synod participant, adds, "From that point of view, individual confession of sins is of enormous importance and value. By this means people are led to focus on the specific reality of their own relationships with God.

"Just as a person would be wasting time to speak in general terms to a doctor about ill health and must instead detail the facts of his or her own symptoms in order to obtain relief, so individuals seeking reconciliation in the sacrament of penance need to bring to bear their best powers of self-analysis as part of their contribution to the healing process." To put that another way, it's questionable whether a person who isn't willing to confess his sins is really sorry for them or, perhaps, even knows very clearly what he ought to be sorry about.

"When a sinner confesses his guilt in confession," says the mystic and spiritual writer Adrienne von Speyr, "there arises a twofold relation between him and his sin: he identifies himself with his sin in recognizing and confessing it, and he affirms himself to be a sinner. And while he acknowledges it as his own and his own exclusively, he sets himself apart from it by his contrition." All of these elements are of the utmost importance. "It is precisely his act of fully accepting his sin in confession and of sorrow for it that leads to its complete removal. The sinner confesses in order that the sin may be taken away. He joins himself with it, in order that he may be freed from it."

But stressing the personal character of sin and reconciliation, and the intimate relationship between the sinner and God, points to another question (and objection) which people sometimes raise concerning the sacrament of penance: Why confess your sins to a priest? If "everything takes place between the individual alone and God," why complicate matters by involving a third party? Why not just say "I'm sorry" to God and let that suffice?

There are two complementary answers.

One concerns the role of the priest as minister of the sacrament. Although it's customary to use the analogy of the doctor-patient relationship to shed light on some aspects of penance, the analogy breaks down at just this point. A doctor giving medical advice represents nobody but himself. A priest administering the sacrament first and foremost represents somebody else: Christ.

But even to say that the priest "represents" Christ falls considerably short of the reality. The traditional way of expressing his role is to say that as minister of the sacrament the priest stands *in persona Christi* — in the person of Christ. Christ, in other words, acts in and through the priest in order to forgive our sins. It's easy to see why the Holy Father speaks of hearing confessions as "undoubtedly the most difficult and sensitive, the most exhausting and demanding ministry of the priest, but also one of the most beautiful and consoling."

The second answer has to do with another important reality about the sacrament of penance: its communal aspect.

It's true that sin is primarily and essentially an offense against God, a disruption in our relationship with him. But it is no less true that sin involves a rupture (ranging from barely perceptible to overwhelmingly obvious) in our relationships with other people. In particular, sin weakens and, if it is serious enough, may even sever the sinner's bonds with the community of faith, the Church. It follows that the Church needs also to be involved in the process of reconciliation.

Obviously it isn't possible or desirable for the whole community of faith to be an immediate party to each act of reconciliation, each individual celebration of penance. But neither is it necessary. Instead, the priest represents the community in administering the sacrament; he is the embodiment, as it were, of the communal aspect of reconciliation. This is true even in the case of communal penance services with individual confession of sins and individual absolution.

"One cannot deny," the pope says, "the social nature of this sacrament, in which the whole Church — militant, suffering, and glorious in heaven — comes to the aid of the penitent and welcomes him again . . . especially as it was the whole Church which had been offended and wounded by his sin. As the minister of penance, the priest, by virtue of his sacred office, appears as the witness and representative of this ecclesial nature of the sacrament."

Arguing the case for the sacrament of penance is evidently necessary at this moment in history, but that fact itself is a strange and disturbing thing. It's a little like having to make the case for taking basic care of your health: the advantages are so evident that it's hard to see why anyone would doubt them in the first place.

As far as the sacrament is concerned,

however, many people today do have their doubts. Perhaps it isn't arguments they need so much as the flash of insight and the experience of living faith which have helped saints and ordinary Christians without number throughout the centuries to see this sacrament for what it is — a remarkable expression of God's loving generosity toward troubled human beings.

The renewal of the sacrament at which Vatican II aimed, Pope John Paul writes, was "meant to stir up in each one of us a new impulse towards the renewal of our interior attitude; towards a deeper understanding of the nature of the sacrament of penance; towards a reception of the sacrament which is more filled with faith, not anxious but trusting; towards a more frequent celebration of the sacrament which is seen to be completely filled with the Lord's merciful love." In other words, the sacrament of penance is necessary not only for forgiveness of sin but also for growth in the love of God. It's to that rewarding subject that we need now to turn.

# CHAPTER 9

# Penance and the Interior Life

Most of what has been said up to now about the sacrament of penance highlights its role in the forgiveness of serious sins. There is, however, another perspective from which to consider the sacrament's "necessity." That is to view it as an indispensable instrument for progress in the interior life.

Here it's usually not a question of confessing because one has committed mortal sin (although that possibility always exists for anyone, no matter how saintly he or she may be), but because one is serious about the pursuit of sanctity. This is why spiritual writers so strongly recommend "confessions of devotion" — that is, regular reception of the sacrament by people who ordinarily have no serious sins to confess but who find in the sacrament of penance pardon for their real but lesser faults along with human and supernatural assistance in seeking spiritual growth.

To understand the role of the sacrament in this context, it is necessary first to sketch the "context" itself — I mean the interior life of an individual (for purposes of this discussion, a lay person) who is serious about trying to become a saint and wishes to adopt the necessary means to that end. At the outset it's important to set aside some false notions on this subject; and here a personal anecdote may help.

Many years ago, I found myself at a Catholic seminary giving a talk on lay spirituality. That I was doing so was a tribute to the indulgent optimism of the friend who'd invited me to speak and to my own erroneous certitude that I would always have something worthwhile to say on any subject, no matter how little I really knew about it.

And what did I say? In effect, that there's no such thing as spirituality for lay people. Priests and religious have the real interior lives. The rest of us can only hope occasionally to remove ourselves from our natural environment — family, job, the world — in order to steal a little time to act like monks and nuns.

Perhaps the biggest problem was this

thing called "the world." As a factor in the life of a Christian, it had only two functions: first, to be a place where you learned to say no — where "doing good" *was* "avoiding evil"; second, as something to be avoided, shunned, fled from as much as possible so that you could lead some kind of poor imitation of the monastic life in whatever scattered corners of time and circumstance you might snatch for the purpose.

A sad caricature, of course, but at least there is one thing to be said in defense of my performance all those years ago: I wasn't the only one who thought that way. I was only parroting what had been for a long time the prevailing Christian view of the world, the spiritual life, and the awkward situation of lay people.

You find this view in many sources — in Saint Augustine, for example, and centuries later in the *Imitation of Christ*. Obviously, Augustine was a genius and a saint, one of the Fathers of the Church and one of the founders of Western civilization, while the *Imitation of Christ* is a spiritual classic. Yet both contain certain strands of thought which, alongside much that is priceless and permanently valid, present a rather skewed and inadequate vision of Christian life in the world.

In the tenth book of his *Confessions*, for instance, Augustine undertakes to define what he calls "the happy life." Not surprisingly, he identifies it entirely and exclusively with God: "There is a joy that is not granted to the wicked, but only to those who worship you for your own sake, and for whom you yourself are joy. This is the happy life, to rejoice over you, to you, and because of you: this it is, and there is no other. Those who think that there is another such life pursue another joy and it is not true joy."

Considering Augustine's personal history — long years of dalliance with false joys followed by one of the most profound and far-reaching conversions in history — it isn't hard to comprehend the origins of this passage. But isn't there something rather out of focus about it?

While leaving the serious argument to philosophers and theologians, I'm not at all sure it is possible, as Augustine seems to suggest, for human beings to choose the Good which is God as such and for its own sake. It isn't necessarily that we don't want to or wouldn't do it if we could. It's simply that we are made in such a way that our choices must concern *human* goods, and, even where God is in question, we approach him (or draw away from him) through the use (or misuse) which we make of creatures. Augustine tries to leap over creatures — to set aside human goods and the choices we make among them as if they were of no account — and to rush directly into the arms of God. This, he says, is the "happy life" for a human being. Perhaps it was for Augustine, but it's by no means clear that such a life is accessible to the rest of us.

Centuries later we find the same sort of thinking in very pure form in the *Imitation of Christ*. Thus: "Oh, this is the highest and safest wisdom, that by contempt of the world we endeavor to please God. . . . And, therefore, wean your heart from all earthly things which are visible and perishable; and turn yourself to the invisible eternal things. For all those who follow their carnal desires defile their conscience and lose the grace of God."

I do not mean to suggest that nothing

true and important is being said here; but there is also something troubling, something that rings false, in so *exclusive* an emphasis on the contempt for the world and the rejection of bodily human goods. It's not just that it's difficult — a way of life and form of spirituality which most lay persons aren't very likely ever to achieve and consistently sustain; but that, if the truth be told, we aren't altogether certain that this particular vision represents an ideal to which we *ought* to aspire. God made the world: are we really meant to turn up our noses at it?

In fact, living as Christians in the world is essential, both for the world and for the Christian laity. For it is a central and indispensable element of the vocation of lay persons that they sanctify themselves in and through their involvement in the secular order, while at the same time contributing to the sanctification of the secular order itself — to that restoration of all things in Christ to which, Christians believe, history is ultimately tending.

This idea of "vocation" is crucial to understanding the nature of Christian life in the world.

For many people, "vocation" signifies only the special calling which draws some people to the priesthood and religious life. Priests and brothers and nuns have vocations. Whereas, as far as the rest of us are concerned, the attitude is roughly this: "Lay people have . . . jobs, I suppose. Families. Commitments and relationships of various kinds. But certainly not vocations."

This way of thinking is both false and dangerous. *Every Christian has a vocation* — not in some weak, accommodated sense, but in a full, literal, and demanding sense. For many centuries one of the great problems of Christian life has been the lack of an adequate understanding of vocation, including precisely the understanding that everybody has one.

Indeed, it might be well if lay people thought of themselves not merely as "having" vocations but as living in an exceptionally rich vocational context. First, there is the common Christian vocation shared by every baptized person — to love and serve God and neighbor and work out one's salvation by doing so. Next, this common calling is further specified by the choice of a state of life — as lay person or priest or religious, as married or single — which carries with it a whole raft of duties and obligations. Finally, an individual's place in the scheme of things receives its ultimate specification through his unique personal vocation — the special role which he, and only he, is called to play in God's plan.

What does "unique personal vocation" mean? Perhaps it might be described as the sum total of who and what I am, with all that it entails as far as moral obligations and apostolic opportunities are concerned. So, for example, I am a husband (of this particular wife), a father (of these particular children), a worker (in this particular job), a writer (of these particular books and articles), a friend (of these particular people), a citizen (of this particular country), a member (of this particular parish, these particular organizations), and so on and on, until I've expressed the whole complex network of roles and commitments and duties which make up my life.

Can all this — the stuff of ordinary life — really be called a vocation? Indeed it can, provided it isn't left merely on the natural level, but is recognized and accepted as my part in God's providential plan, and is directed to the apostolate — or, more precisely, to seeking out and finding the apostolic purposes which this network of roles and commitments has in God's eyes. In regard to every element of my life, I am meant to seek and do God's precise will *for me*, to find the means God offers *me* for continuing his redemptive work in Jesus and helping to restore all things in Christ.

It is at this point that the idea and practice of penance — very much including reception of the sacrament itself — become relevant from the perspective we've now adopted. It is not necessarily an easy thing to discern a personal vocation, especially since the work of learning precisely what God wants of me is not something to be done once and for all, but is a constant, daily task. My own weakness, self-will, and sinfulness often barge in, confusing me and turning me down false paths. And, if discernment is difficult, still harder at many times (and generally at just those times when it is most important) is living up to the specific entailments of the vocation I've discerned; indeed, I often fail to do so, and each failure supplies a new inducement and rationalization to give up the effort entirely.

Here, then, the sacrament of penance plays its indispensable role, clearing away the obstacles to discernment, bringing me God's pardon for my failures to live up to his will for me, encouraging me in my renewed efforts to live my vocation, shielding me against the insidious temptation to stop trying.

In what does sanctity consist? Evidently, in doing the duties that belong to our own lives — responding to our unique personal vocations — with great love of God and neighbor. For some this may mean performing visibly dramatic deeds; for most it will mean leading hidden lives, but investing their diverse elements with such intense love that the result is spiritually heroic.

But living this way doesn't come easily. Two things are necessary: a personal plan for the nurturing of a healthy spiritual life and perseverance in carrying out the plan. Otherwise, talk about sanctity is idle chatter.

Here, too, the sacrament of penance is

crucially important — a central element in the plan of life of one who is striving for sanctity. It occupies this place because, even for such a person, falls are frequent and the need for help in constantly beginning again is very great. Penance is one of the most important means given us by Christ for growth in the interior life. It is also a necessary corrective tool, which helps curb our ever-present tendency to deviate from the course we have set ourselves and brings us God's forgiveness for the many times we do.

To do them credit, Saint Augustine and the *Imitation of Christ* were overwhelmingly correct in this: as a result of sin, both original sin and personal sin, there is a great deal of evil in the world and in us. Penance is necessary for one who wishes to seek sanctity in the face of that otherwise discouraging fact.

# CHAPTER 10

## Plan of Life

At first the idea of making the sacrament of penance part of a formal plan for the interior life may sound strange and unappealing. The difficulty may have to do with the sacrament, but it may just as well have to do with the very notion of a plan. "Shouldn't spontaneity predominate here?" someone will object. "Why try to regiment spirituality by a preconceived plan?"

The objection misses the point. A plan for the interior life doesn't enforce conformity but provides a framework for creativity. Here if anywhere we need to put aside illusions and be painfully honest with ourselves: human nature being what it is, spontaneity without discipline doesn't lead to creativity — it leads to sloppiness, erratic behavior, and sooner or later to the cessation of effort.

A plan of life necessarily includes a number of different "activities." Among these are Mass and Communion, personal prayer, Scripture and spiritual reading, and acts of mortification intended to conquer the tendency toward sin. Penance — reception of the sacrament and penitential practices — also plays a large role, both in its own right and in relation to other elements of the plan.

To have maximum benefit, it's important that these not remain isolated, individual practices. They should be integrated and oriented toward an overall purpose: establishing, maintaining, and constantly deepening one's relationship with God.

There are various ways to express that. One, which calls attention to the context of everyday life, is to speak of the "presence of God." The aim is to live constantly with an awareness of God (more or less intense at different times, of course) and with the intention of doing his will. The elements of a spiritual plan can help make this sense of God's abiding presence in our lives an achievable reality rather than an attractive but unreachable ideal.

But even though the interior life of a Christian is essentially concerned with his or her relationship with God, if that is *all* there is to be said about it, there's something lacking even in that relationship. One's relationship with God cannot be isolated from one's relationships with other people, and the ultimate test of how well one has loved the Lord will be how well one has loved other human beings.

Jesus testifies to that in a powerful passage in Matthew's Gospel. At the Last Judgment, he says, the just and the unjust alike will ask Christ, whom they never saw during life, when it was that they responded — or failed to respond — to him. And Jesus will answer: "I assure you, as often as you did it for one of my least brothers, you did it for me. . . . As often as you neglected to do it to one of these least ones, you neglected to do it to me" (Matthew 25:40, 45).

We must do good to others, and the greatest good we can do them is to share with them God's truth and love, which we have received as an unmerited gift. We must not merely keep the faith but spread it abroad for the liberation of the world. This is the meaning of what is called the Christian apostolate.

"Apostolate" does not signify some out-of-the-ordinary activity, reserved to a few people specially designated for the purpose. Precisely this notion has done harm in the past, helping to reinforce the belief that priests and religious are the only people who have serious roles in carrying out the mission of Christ and his Church. One consequence, often enough, has been to foster passivity and noninvolvement on the part of lay people.

It is a true and exceedingly important fact (which today is fairly often ignored, denied, or otherwise muddled up) that clergy, religious, and laity have specifically different functions in the Church. Saint Paul, among others, is very clear about the differentiation of roles within the Mystical Body. But all members of the Church — clergy, religious, and laity — share in the basic Christian vocation by reason of their baptism; and in large measure this is a vocation to the apostolate. Here is Paul on the whole matter:

> Just as each one of us has one
> body with many members, and not all
> the members have the same function,
> so too we, though many, are one body

in Christ and individually members one of another. We have gifts that differ according to the favor bestowed on each of us. One's gift may be prophecy; its use should be in proportion to his faith. It may be the gift of ministry; it should be used for service. One who is a teacher should use his gift for teaching; one with the power of exhortation should exhort. He who gives alms should do so generously; he who rules should exercise his authority with care; he who performs works of mercy should do so cheerfully.

— Romans 12:4-8

Fundamentally, the concept of apostolate means continuing Jesus' work in our world today. It is not a task reserved for special people in special circumstances. It doesn't pertain only to Sunday and to "churchy" settings. Everyone should carry out his or her share of the Christian apostolate according to the circumstances of his or her life — at home, in the neighborhood, at school, on the job. All these are places where Christ wishes to be present; but that will only happen if dedicated Christians make him present there.

It would be wrong, however, to give a painfully "pious" impression of the apostolate; while it takes many forms, one which it almost certainly does *not* take is pulling a long face, indulging in preachy talk, and handing out religious tracts.

On the contrary, the apostolate will usually begin with the most natural thing in the world — friendship. Christians who wish to live apostolically must get to know other people, enter into their lives, share their sorrows and their joys, look for ways of extending them encouragement and support to cope with their manifold needs and challenges.

Then, perhaps, times will come when the Christian apostolate can naturally move to a different, deeper plane: a word spoken to a friend who stopped practicing his religion years ago; a serious conversation with a fellow worker who acknowledges her uncertainties about the meaning of life; some practical suggestions for a neighbor who thinks he might like to work harder at improving his relationship with God but doesn't know where or how to begin.

This suggests a special and, today, much needed form of apostolate: encouraging Catholics who have more or less given up receiving the sacrament of penance to return to confession. In years gone by, relatives and friends spontaneously worried about "lapsed" Catholics who stayed away from the sacrament and often tried to get them to mend their ways; no doubt the same thing still happens today, yet hardly so often when even "practicing" Catholics make it a practice to neglect penance. Those in whose lives the sacrament of penance still plays a strong, vital part shouldn't keep the good news to themselves but should make advocacy for the sacrament a part of their apostolic program.

Where the apostolate in all its diverse forms is in question, the clergy and religious cannot do it all. There aren't enough of them, and they cannot enter into every corner of the secular world and every situation in daily life. To bring Christ into all these settings demands the best effort of all Christians. *That* is what the apostolate is all about.

Not only is the apostolate a necessary part of the plan of life for serious Christians, but the other elements of the plan provide the strength and encouragement — the spiritual calories, as it were — for diligent and persevering apostolic activity. This, as we shall see, is eminently true of the sacrament of penance.

Obviously the Mass has a central place in any such plan. Yet, as with a lot of pious remarks, this particular one has been repeated so often that it's a temptation to tune it out when we hear it yet again: "The Mass is the center of our lives as Christians." What does that really mean? In what sense is it true? Putting aside the many explanations we've all heard up to now, let's take a fresh look at the Eucharist and its significance in our lives.

The most important fact about the Mass is this: here Christ renews the act by which he redeemed us and makes it possible for us to take part in that act. The core of his "act" is a human choice, a decision: to be absolutely faithful to the will of his Father in all things but especially in the carrying out of his mission as Redeemer — to which everything else in his life was oriented — no matter what the consequences for himself.

This choice of Christ's was executed preeminently at the Last Supper, which he shared with his apostles. Aware that he faced death, he could have fled; instead he pursued his calling to give glory to the Father to its ultimate conclusion. At that meal, moreover, he specifically commissioned the apostles and those who would come after them to reaffirm and renew the act of fidelity which he then expressed and celebrated. His commitment was brought to completion the following day, Good Friday, in his suffering and death on Calvary. This complex act of Jesus' was, and was intended by him to be, redemptive: it took away our sins.

The Mass is quite rightly said to be a sacrifice and a meal. But essentially it is the continued execution of a human choice — Jesus' choice of redemptive fidelity. We see how this can be possible by considering that any choice, once made, lasts and can be renewed until canceled by a contrary choice. Plainly, however, Jesus will never reverse his decision to be faithful to the Father's will and thereby redeem us. That choice endures; and he expresses it once more in every Eucharist to the end of time.

More than that, he makes it possible for us to participate in his act — to unite our weak and imperfect efforts to be faithful to God's will, and so to cooperate in our redemption from sin, with his perfect act of commitment. In this sense the Mass is indeed the center of our lives as Christians: it is an organizing principle of Christian life, not just in general terms but, potentially at least, on a day-to-day basis.

There are several reasons for that. For one thing, in order to celebrate the Mass well, we must live authentic Christian lives. The Eucharist reaffirms Jesus' redemptive choice and offers us the opportunity to join him in this act of fidelity and, in so doing, affirm our intention to cooperate in our redemption from sin. But if our lives are not in harmony with what we propose to express by participation in the Mass, it will scarcely be a very rewarding experience for us.

People sometimes complain that they "don't get much out of Mass." There are a number of possible explanations, including carelessly celebrated liturgies and badly preached homilies. But one reason is that some people do not prepare for the Eucharist by leading lives which express what it proclaims and celebrates. The Mass is not magic. Those few minutes do not and cannot compensate for days, weeks, and even years of infidelity to God's will.

The Eucharist, it must be remembered, is Christ's sacrifice to take away our sins. That is good reason for thanksgiving and rejoicing to be part of our attitude toward the Eucharist. But participation in Christ's redemptive act also necessarily requires penance as a precondition. People in whose lives sin remains a reality (and is there anyone in whose life it does *not*?) but who seldom or never confront and acknowledge their sinfulness, repent it, and beg God's pardon, have simply not prepared themselves to take part in Jesus' redemptive act. At best, the Mass for them is likely to be a kind of pious show — as good as, but no better than, the quality of the homily, the singing, and the flowers on the altar.

For those, however, who do strive to live authentic Christian lives, even in the face of their weakness and repeated failure, the Mass is a genuine organizing principle of everyday life. In the course of a day, such people prepare, as it were, the material which they will join with Christ's offering to the Father at the next Eucharist.

This "material" is simply the content of their lives, lived to the best of their ability in a spirit of redemptive fidelity to God's will for them. Inevitably, of course, these are also lives in which sin is present to some degree; but so, too, along with sin, are the acknowledgment of sin, sorrow, and the true experience of God's pardon — especially and regularly in the sacrament of penance — together with constantly renewed efforts to be faithful to the form which God's will takes for them in their personal vocations. The mutual love and support of a married couple, the generous self-giving of parents in service to their children, the honest carrying out of their duties by working people, the serious pursuit of knowledge by students, the pastoral sensitivity of priests, the daily work and prayers of religious, the patiently accepted suffering of sick persons — these are the "ordinary" elements of life which we can bring with us to the Eucharist to be lifted up to the Father in union with Jesus' act of loving, redemptive fidelity.

But there is still more to it than that. At Mass we are strengthened by receiving the Blessed Sacrament — that is, by being united with Christ himself, incredibly accessible to us as nourishment for our struggle to overcome sin and live Christian lives. The pattern is circular: our lives as Christians are oriented to participation in the Eucharist and also flow from it. Christian life is eucharistic life.

Perhaps this suggests an answer to the question "How often should I go to Mass?" A person for whom the Mass is the organizing principle of life will participate in the Eucharist as often as possible — daily if that can be done, but in any case frequently and regularly.

Even more frequently it is necessary that we pray. There are two classic definitions of prayer — lifting the mind and heart to God, and conversation with God. Both say something useful and true about prayer, but perhaps the second is the more enlightening, since it makes clear prayer's functional role in the interior life.

Communication is essential to any relationship. Since the purpose of the interior life is to establish, maintain, and strengthen a relationship with God, communication with God — prayer — is essential to it.

In very general terms, we can identify two different kinds of prayer. One is vocal prayer — the prayer of words and formulae: the Our Father, the Hail Mary, and so on. The other is mental prayer. Each has an important role to play; neither can be neglected.

At the outset, people usually find mental prayer the more difficult. Indeed, its difficulty discourages some from attempting to pray in this way or from persevering in the effort. That is a serious mistake, for the effort itself is important and is pleasing to God.

Admittedly, "mental prayer" sounds forbidding, something that mystics do, but not ordinary people like the rest of us. In fact, however, mental prayer is possible not just for mystics but for anyone who cares to try.

How to begin? Perhaps with a very simple statement: "Lord, I don't know how to pray." That also is a prayer, and it has been the starting point of a rich and rewarding life of prayer for many people.

There are numerous techniques for mental prayer, but the best advice is to do what one finds helpful and ignore what doesn't help. Probably it's best at the start not to become burdened with theories and techniques. God wants us to converse with him, and he will help us if we try.

Nevertheless, it is useful to keep a few practical points in mind. For example, it's usually necessary to start mental prayer by making a deliberate effort to shift the focus from immediate concerns to God. Reading something — a passage from Scripture, perhaps — can be helpful, besides providing material for prayer.

Mental prayer comes from the heart. We can use words if we wish, but they are not essential. With or without words, it is necessary to open oneself to God, express what is really in one's heart, and seek his light and help. The subject matter of prayer need not be "edifying" in stereotyped terms; we should talk to God about what is really on our minds, not what we think ideally should be there.

Certainly this is a time for acts of love and gratitude and trust, and also for acts of sorrow and reparation, both for our own sins and for the sins of others. This latter emphasis in prayer is natural and necessary. Prayer is part of a process of growth which involves constant conversion — constant turning away from sin and turning to God. Penance therefore has an important place in prayer, and our continuing conversation with God very naturally leads to and also flows from reception of the sacrament of penance. For penance, both sacramental and nonsacramental, is like a sturdy thread running throughout the complex but unified tapestry which is the interior life of a Christian.

One method of prayer, accessible to almost everyone, is what is called centering prayer. In this form of prayer, one tries simply to relax, set aside distractions, and concentrate on God's presence and his goodness, expressing loving gratitude for all he is and does for us and trustful sorrow for the inadequacy of one's own response. In a certain sense, nothing happens in such prayer — one just "wastes time" with God — but this "wasting time" is an experience of spiritual refreshment.

It shouldn't be made to sound too easy, though. There are difficulties in mental prayer, and sooner or later anyone who attempts to pray encounters them. One of the most common is dryness — the absence of consolation, the feeling that one is merely going through the motions without accomplishing anything.

This experience is not in itself a sign of failure. Great saints have reported the same, often for years on end. It is God's way of simultaneously testing us and encouraging us to persevere: the sense of his absence is, paradoxically, an incentive to continue seeking him. Almost anyone can pray now and then, especially at times of crisis and great need. It is saints who pray perseveringly, in season and out, when prayer comes easily and also when it doesn't. The measure of "good" prayer is not the emotional satisfaction we happen to take from it, but our perseverance; the only failure would be to abandon the effort.

Mental prayer requires a specific period of time set aside every day for this purpose and nothing else. By contrast, vocal prayer is possible in many different circumstances. It enables us to fill the day with prayer.

One of the best of all vocal prayers is the Rosary. Its familiar "mysteries" are matter for short meditations through which we grow in understanding and appreciation of central episodes in the lives of Jesus, Mary, and Joseph. As a prayer particularly associated with the Blessed Virgin, the Rosary deepens our devotion to her and thus associates us closely with our best, most reliable guide to the life of the spirit.

One thing helpful — indeed, very nearly indispensable — to perseverance in prayer is spiritual reading. This is not surprising when we reflect on its role in the interior life.

Rule out two things at the start: information and entertainment. Of course, if something we read does inform or entertain us, so much the better; no one is likely to profit from spiritual reading which he finds obscure or unbearably dull. But the focus of this particular exercise is somewhere else. Spiritual reading is directly linked to prayer, and its purpose is to supply material for our conversations with God.

In that respect spiritual reading is not

greatly different from reading a newspaper and then chatting with a spouse or friend about what we've read. In these cases, too, reading serves as an instrument for building up relationships. That suggests why, technically speaking, it is even a little misleading to speak of spiritual "reading." Although for most people reading is involved, the same purpose can be, and often is, served by "hearing" (the proclamation of God's word) or even "seeing" (images — the crucifix is a good example — which provide us with food for thought, stir up devotion, and lead us to prayer). "Spiritual reading" is no elitist activity.

The preeminent reading matter for all Christians is God's word as it comes to us in the Bible. For if prayer is a conversation with God, where does one turn to find God's side of the conversation? In fact, he speaks to us in many ways — through events, through family, friends, and associates, through the teaching of the Church, even through direct promptings that may come to us at the time of prayer itself. But especially he speaks to us in Sacred Scripture. Thus, an excellent pattern for prayer is to begin with thoughtful, reflective reading of the Bible in order to hear God's word, and to follow this with one's own response — the thoughts, affections, and resolutions which God's word inspires.

There are also many excellent books for spiritual reading in addition to, though certainly not in place of, the Bible. While good spiritual literature is being written and published today, it is important not to neglect the classics in the field, which have stood the test of time and transcended trendiness and faddishness.

This is not the place for a long list of books, but a few titles deserve mention. For example — and in partial amends for some remarks made earlier — it should be noted that Christians for centuries have used the *Imitation of Christ*, by Thomas à Kempis. Although the book is a product of its time, and the spirituality it recommends is not totally suited to the needs of Christians living in today's world, everyone will find something of lasting benefit here.

Somewhat closer to modern times is *The Introduction to the Devout Life*, by Saint Francis de Sales. Written especially for lay people, it remains a practical treatment of lay spirituality.

Also directed to Christians in the world, and thoroughly modern in tone and approach, is *The Way*, by Monsignor Josemaría Escrivá de Balaguer. This is a collection of short spiritual maxims, well suited for use in connection with mental prayer, which deal in direct, colloquial terms with the issues and concerns which typically arise in the daily life of one seeking sanctity.

Another excellent modern introduction to the interior life is *This Tremendous Lover*, by Dom Eugene Boylan. This work deals systematically with the theory and the practice of spirituality in a way which both beginners and those who are more experienced can profit from. Boylan's *Difficulties in Mental Prayer* is an exemplary short introduction to methods and attitudes in prayer.

Saints' lives set forth models for the pursuit of sanctity, and some saints have given their own accounts of their pilgrimages — for example, Saint Augustine in his *Confessions* (the first, autobiographical half of the book, that is) and Saints Teresa of Ávila and Thérèse of Lisieux, two strikingly different personalities who scaled the heights of sanctity.

Fairly recent writers like G.K. Chesterton and Cardinal John Henry Newman have produced many works which are of high literary quality besides being excellent spiritual reading. Nor should we neglect the documents of Vatican Council II (the *Dogmatic Constitution on the Church* and the *Pastoral Constitution on the Church in the Modern World* are especially meaty) and encyclicals like Pope John Paul II's *On Human Work* and *Rich in Mercy*. The style of conciliar and papal documents tends to be heavy, but the content is excellent.

How much time should go to spiritual reading? It's more important to do it regularly — daily if possible — than at great length. Fifteen minutes a day, divided between Scripture and some other book, is suitable for most people. Practiced in conjunction with prayer, it can help immensely.

These, then, are some of the elements of a plan of life *into which* the sacrament of penance fits. Now we'll look more closely at the sacrament itself in this particular context.

# CHAPTER 11

# Penance and Sanctity

For serious Christians (who, it should be noted, are by no means the same thing as solemn Christians and least of all the same as stuffy Christians), the ultimate aim of a plan of life is sanctity. It is thus in reference to the quest for sanctity that the sacrament of penance, as part of a plan of life, should be understood.

But not just penance in isolation. The sacrament sheds light on, and is in turn illuminated by, two other practices: examination of conscience and what is called the "particular examination." All three, finally, are best considered in the context of spiritual direction.

Quite a lot has just been said, and all of it needs some explaining. Let's begin, then, with the notion of spiritual direction. Most people who have thought seriously about sanctity and how to pursue it agree that spiritual direction is necessary for anyone who wants to make significant progress in the interior life.

It isn't hard to see why. We routinely consult other people in other areas of our lives, on the sound principle that our subjective opinions need to be supplemented by the informed, objective views of others. We see doctors about our physical health, lawyers about our legal affairs, mechanics about our cars, and so on. It is not so different in the spiritual life. A prudent person will use a counselor in his or her efforts to achieve sanctity. This adviser's role is not "direction" in the sense of giving orders; rather, he is a friend and a guide — someone who knows us well and puts his own experience of the interior life at our disposal as we seek to find our way.

Reception of the sacrament of penance, examination of conscience, and the practice called particular examination all fit extremely well into spiritual direction. It is not that these practices are impossible apart from it; but in most cases they will produce maximum benefit when they are elements of the process known broadly as direction.

Penance and examination of conscience clearly go together: self-examination is a necessary part of the preparation for the sacrament. But examination of conscience should not be just an occasional activity in immediate preparation for confession. Instead, it should be a regular, daily part of one's plan of life.

Obviously this doesn't mean a prolonged, possibly morbid exercise in self-examination. A quick but reasonably thorough check according to some predetermined plan is ordinarily sufficient. Where did I miss the target today? How can I do better tomorrow? Then a quick word of sorrow to God and a prayer for his help — and the examination is completed.

The point of this is precisely to be as realistic and accurate as possible about our spiritual selves. Daily examination of conscience takes the process of self-assessment out of the realm of an occasional, impressionistic overview and helps us come to grips with small problems before they become large ones.

So in its own way does the practice called particular examination. This traditional spiritual exercise is an "examination" in the sense that it requires us to reflect on ourselves — our strengths and weaknesses, our virtues and vices — and come to know ourselves better. It is "particular" because it zeroes in on something specific — some virtue to acquire, some bad habit to overcome. It does this furthermore by proposing some very concrete practice in order to achieve the desired result.

For instance, a student who determined to work harder at school might as his "particular examination" set himself a definite schedule dividing his time between study and recreation. A husband determined to be kinder to his wife might decide as his "particular examination" to do the dishes every night. The point of the exercise is to identify an area where improvement is needed and then adopt a very specific way of improving.

Here, too, the advice of a prudent spiritual director who knows us well is of inestimable value. Examination of conscience, the sacrament of penance, and the particular examination: each in its own way helps us to overcome weaknesses and grow in the interior life. The assistance of a spiritual guide is an enormous advantage in that effort.

Penitential practices and mortification

are likewise appropriate elements of a plan of life, as well as apt matters for discussion in spiritual direction. Yet even to speak of "penitential practices and mortification" can attract unfavorable attention these days. Penance and mortification are under a cloud, suspected of being morbid and unhealthy. Surely nobody wants to bring back hair shirts!

As a matter of fact, I don't. But there is something lacking, even unbalanced, in a notion of Christian life which allows no room for penance and mortification. These practices have been part of Christian thinking about the pursuit of sanctity too long for us to imagine now that we can casually set them aside without doing ourselves injury.

There are in fact excellent reasons, having to do with the living of Christian life, for penance and mortification. Let's start with this thing called mortification.

Literally, mortification signifies dying to self, but less literally it refers to those practices, physical and spiritual, undertaken in a systematic campaign against mortal and venial sin in oneself. Thus, it signifies dying to sin and in this way coming to life — the life of fulfillment in Christ.

The tendency which people have today to look askance at anything called mortification makes little sense. For this practice is best understood as a form of self-discipline, and often the very people who decry mortification for spiritual health can be seen mortifying themselves furiously through intensive exercise undertaken for the sake of physical health.

Mortification and asceticism are intended to accomplish something rather similar on the spiritual level. If the contradiction can be tolerated, they might be thought of as spiritual body-building. The aim is to develop the powers of will and self-control in small matters, so that, when larger challenges arise, one will be able to cope with them successfully.

Good mortifications are of many kinds. Passing up a favorite food is a typical example, but there are also subtler mortifications of an emotional, psychological sort — for instance, leaving a joke untold, deliberately not having the last word in a discussion, going out of one's way to be pleasant to a

146

person one finds irritating. Whatever form they take, good mortifications do not mortify other people. If the result of some small practice we've identified for ourselves is to make us disagreeable and hard to get along with, it's probably best to abandon that particular practice and find another one.

Although penitential practices are very much like mortification, the emphasis here is slightly different. Penance carries the suggestion of "making up" for something. But what we most need to make up for is sin, our own and others'; and a traditional name for this is reparation.

Absolutely speaking, of course, *we* cannot make up for the offense against God involved in any sin. When God forgives sin, it is not because we have done something which requires it; his forgiveness springs totally from his own gracious generosity.

Still, penitential practices — fasting and abstaining, say, or positive acts of charity done in the name of penance — are small, tangible expressions of sorrow and the disposition to receive God's forgiveness. They do not extort anything from God, but we can be sure they please him.

The penance performed after receiving the sacrament of penance, that is, after our sins have been forgiven, is similarly important. This "satisfaction" for sin teaches sin's seriousness, serves as a deterrent to future sin, contributes to healing the injury to self which the sinner does by sin, and assists in overcoming the bad habits of sinful living. True, the small penances typically assigned are mere tokens of sorrow and reparation; but for one who has a spirit of penance, all of life's sufferings can contribute to this enterprise of making satisfaction for sins.

At its deepest level, penance has a meaning which is hard to fathom yet profoundly significant. Saint Paul, in his letter to the Colossians (1:24), expresses it this way: "In my own flesh I fill up what is lacking in the sufferings of Christ for the sake of his body, the church."

It hardly needs saying that Paul did not speak of what was "lacking" in Christ's suffering in any pejorative sense. Christ's suffering is perfectly, universally redemptive in its own right. Yet, from a human point of view, it is obvious that Christ did not exhaust human suffering. Other men and women suffer, too; *we* suffer. What meaning can we find in our sufferings, whether they be voluntary or involuntary? Paul suggests the answer.

Membership in Christ's Mystical Body, the Church, makes it possible for us to put suffering to good use, as it were — to participate in the very suffering of Christ and to "fill up what is lacking" in his sufferings. We do this, simply, by intending it — either by turning our involuntary sufferings to this end or by voluntarily seeking sufferings, small penances, with this end in view.

Participation in the suffering of Christ is a great mystery. It is also a privileged fact of Christian life and membership in Christ's Mystical Body, which points, among other things, to the response Christians are called to make to evil.

At first, this may seem obvious enough — avoid evil, shun it, and avoid and shun circumstances likely to lead one into evil deeds. As far as it goes, that is excellent advice. But there is also more to be said about evil than simply, "Don't do it."

Specifically, in reflecting upon evil,

Christians are meant to see themselves as co-redeemers with Christ. Classic Christian sources like Saint Augustine and the *Imitation of Christ* are quite correct in emphasizing the presence in the world — and in the human heart — of an enormous amount of evil. But the response Christians are called to make is not to *flee* the world but redeem it. "The great mission that we have received in baptism," says Monsignor Josemaría Escrivá de Balaguer, "is to redeem the world with Christ."

How are we to do that? The only possible answer is that we are to do it as Christ did. It was Jesus' mission as Redeemer to overcome evil; and he accomplished this by perfect fidelity to the will of the Father — fidelity for which, in the end, evil was visited upon him. In some small way, according to the circumstances of our lives, this also is the necessary pattern for people who presume to call themselves Christians. The cross is the symbol of Christianity, not merely in memory of Christ, but as a twofold reminder to us: *that* we are to follow him and *how* we are to follow him.

* * *

Penitential practices and mortification may very well lead to or flow from reception of the sacrament of penance, but in no sense do they substitute for it. Let us now concentrate on the sacrament, considered as part of the plan of life of a person who is serious about the pursuit of sanctity.

Penance is the sacramental action in which we directly encounter Christ for the specific purpose of receiving forgiveness of our sins and strength for our future efforts. Its importance in the case of absolute necessity — serious sin, that is — is obvious. More to the point here, however, the sacrament of penance is also necessary for one who is striving to deepen his or her interior life.

Serious sin may seldom be in question for such a person, but sin and weakness darken everyone's life. There is no better way of coping with our frailty and receiving Christ's pardon and encouragement than this sacrament.

These purposes are best served when the sacrament of penance is part of the process of spiritual direction. Then the benefits are magnified and brought to focus with great specificity upon our spiritual needs and condition. To put it another way, this sacrament is a remarkably effective tool in the hands of a skilled spiritual director.

Not surprisingly, Pope John Paul places great emphasis on the sacrament in his document following up on the 1983 synod of bishops. In doing so, he sets forth a number of fresh and creative considerations. If, as he remarks, the sacrament of penance today is in a certain sense "in crisis" (though, to be sure, the crisis is not with the sacrament but with those who neglect it), serious reflection on what he says can help resolve that unfortunate situation.

On the crucial matter of the confession of sins the Holy Father writes:

> The confession of sins is required, first of all, because the sinner must be known by the person who in the sacrament exercises the role of judge. He has to evaluate both the seriousness of the sins and the repentance of the penitent; he also exercises the role of healer, and must acquaint himself with the condition of the sick person in order to treat and heal him. But the

individual confession also has the value of a sign: a sign of the meeting of the sinner with the mediation of the Church in the person of the minister; a sign of the person's revealing of self as a sinner in the sight of God and the Church, of facing his own sinful condition in the eyes of God.

"The confession of sins," Pope John Paul tells us, "therefore cannot be reduced to a mere attempt at psychological self-liberation." This undoubtedly is true — although one is reminded, at the same time, of the recent observation of a German psychologist, Albert Görres, that "from the psychological point of view, the abandonment of personal confession is a great loss and a grave damage because of the fact that unbiased help is needed to treat guilt and feelings of guilt." Far more than that, however, the sacrament of penance is, as the pope remarks, "a liturgical act," at once signifying and effecting the interaction of human sorrow and divine mercy.

The Holy Father expands on this by telling us:

It is the act of the Prodigal Son who returns to his Father and is welcomed by him with the kiss of peace. It is an act of honesty and courage. It is an act of entrusting oneself, beyond sin, to the mercy that forgives. Thus we understand why the confession of sins must ordinarily be individual and not collective, just as sin is a deeply personal matter. But at the same time confession in a way forces sin out of the secret of the heart and thus out of the area of pure individuality, emphasizing its social character as well, for through the minister of penance it is the ecclesial community, which has been wounded by sin, that welcomes anew the repentant and forgiven sinner.

Unquestionably, Pope John Paul says, it is reconciliation with God which is "the most precious result" of the sacrament of penance. But just as all sin essentially disrupts, to one degree or another, the harmony which ought to exist both within us and in all of our external, interpersonal relationships

— with other human beings as well as with God — so the reconciliation with God which takes place in this sacrament also leads to "other reconciliations, which repair the breaches caused by sin." He goes on to say: "The forgiven penitent is reconciled with himself in his inmost being, where he regains his own true identity. He is reconciled with his brethren whom he has in some way attacked and wounded. He is reconciled with the Church. He is reconciled with all creation."

The Holy Father continues: "Every confessional is a special and blessed place from which, with divisions wiped away, there is born new and uncontaminated a reconciled individual — a reconciled world!"

* * *

Depending on how one looks at it, sanctity is a very simple thing or something very complex. It is simple because ultimately it consists in nothing more than loving God and neighbor — but doing so, of course, to a heroic degree. It is complex because of the almost infinite variety of ways in which love of God and neighbor needs to be expressed in the lives of particular individuals. From that

155

point of view, there are as many different ways of being a saint as there are people.

I was reminded of this not so long ago while rereading, after many years, the autobiography of Saint Thérèse of Lisieux, *The Story of a Soul*. Like sanctity itself, the story it tells is both simple and complex.

Thérèse is one of the greatest and most popular saints of modern times. Yet her way of being a saint embodies, I suspect, a "style" of holiness not much in vogue in some circles today. The autobiography suggests why.

It has to do in part with what could be mistaken for sentimentality. That is perhaps especially true of the name — the "little flower" — by which Thérèse often refers to herself in her book. In context, "little flower" is a perfectly valid figure of speech which expresses the essential spiritual truths — humility and absolute dependence on God — which she grasped and practiced so well. Taken out of context, though, the name probably has a somewhat saccharine sound to today's more cynical ears.

But the matter goes deeper than that. For Thérèse was a holy woman who outwardly led a very circumscribed life and accomplished nothing to speak of. A middle-class upbringing in a provincial French town, nine years in a Carmelite monastery, death when she was only twenty-four — that sums it up. Where, one might ask, could there be room for heroic sanctity in a life like that?

The answer, I believe, confirms the lasting importance of Thérèse of Lisieux.

Thérèse never set out to do visibly great deeds. She admired and prayed fervently for those who did — the missionaries, the apostles of charity, the doers and the activists — but she chose something different for herself, something she considered more suited to a "very little soul." She called it the "little way" — "the way of spiritual childhood, the way of trust and absolute self-surrender." That was the heart of the matter for her. It should be for us, too.

In practical terms, the quest for sanctity lies in doing the duties of one's state of life and responding to the challenges of one's personal vocation with immense love of God and neighbor. For some this means performing dramatic deeds. For others — perhaps most people — it means, as it did with Thérèse, living a hidden life but investing its elements with such great love that the result is spiritually heroic.

It is no coincidence and no mistake that the Church now recognizes as the patrons of the missions Saint Francis Xavier, the Jesuit missionary who carried the faith to the Far East in the sixteenth century, and Saint Thérèse of Lisieux, the nineteenth-century Carmelite nun who went almost nowhere and apparently did almost nothing. Love is the key to sanctity, and sanctity is the lifeblood of the Church, accomplishing wonders by bringing God's grace into human life. There are different kinds of saints but no unimportant ones. And, as we learn from Thérèse of Lisieux, by love the "very little" souls among us can be the greatest.

Love, however, is not necessarily an easy thing either to acquire or to sustain — at least, not when one thinks of "love" not as romantic passion (which comes and goes) but as a settled disposition of the will directed to the service of God and our fellow human beings. Love in this sense demands perseverance — often in the face of one's own disinclination and weakness — and perseverance requires a plan of life, more or less along the lines sketched here and involving as a central element regular and frequent reception of the sacrament of penance.

Even those who wish to love often fail to do so or else love most imperfectly. We sin, and, even when we are not sinning, we blunder repeatedly. In the sacrament of penance Jesus pardons our sins and straightens our paths. To judge by the evidence, many Catholics today have concluded that, for the most part, they can do without the sacrament of penance. They are wrong to think so, and almost certainly they love less well because of their mistake.